Supercharging Node.js Applications with Sequelize

Create high-quality Node.js apps effortlessly while interacting with your SQL database

Daniel Durante

BIRMINGHAM—MUMBAI

Supercharging Node.js Applications with Sequelize

Associate Group Product Manager: Pavan Ramchandani

Publishing Product Manager: Kushal Dave

Senior Editor: Mark Dsouza

Content Development Editor: Divya Vijayan

Technical Editor: Simran Ali

Copy Editor: Safis Editing

Project Coordinator: Sonam Pandey

Proofreader: Safis Editing

Indexer: Pratik Shirodkar

Production Designer: Aparna Bhagat

Marketing Coordinator: Anamika Singh and Marylou De Mello

First published: October 2022

Production reference: 2061222

Published by Packt Publishing Ltd.
Livery Place
35 Livery Street
Birmingham
B3 2PB, UK.

ISBN 978-1-80181-155-2

www.packt.com

To my parents, brother, family, and friends. To Audrey, for teaching me that not all stories have to be boring. To those who have built all of the libraries, frameworks, and applications for making this book possible.

– Daniel J. Durante

Foreword

Sequelize is a modern ORM that supports many different SQL dialects. Sequelize was born during the early days of the JavaScript runtime Node.js. It was the first of its kind, and was presented as a tool for the Node.js community to connect against existing relational databases, or to embrace them in new projects despite the rising trend of document stores. Ever since its release, a strong team of driven engineers added battle-tested support for transactions, relations, eager/lazy loading, read replication, and so much more. Twelve years on, the Sequelize project is part of npm's top 100, and sees wide adoption by huge enterprises and small pet projects alike.

Daniel Durante joined the team in 2013 and contributed immensely to the library's Postgres support by improving the general stability, but also via features such as HStore capabilities and pooling. Furthermore, and maybe most importantly, he was also the one behind the introduction of hooks and object lifecycles, which is now one of the core mechanics used to interact with data objects.

This book will guide you through all the steps of app development, starting with the very ideation of an app, to the modeling of entities and definition of business requirements, all the way to the implementation and deployment of a project. Throughout this journey you'll learn how to grow a small pet project into a stable and scalable application that is free of unwanted side-effects, that caters for auditing of user actions, and can be easily extended going forward.

Enjoy your ride and welcome to the world of databases!

Sascha Depold

Author of Sequelize, Creator of bitte.kaufen and Engineering Manager at eBay

Contributors

About the author

Daniel Durante has nearly a decade of experience in creating Node.js applications with Sequelize. He is currently working on setting up applications and infrastructures for blockchain and options trading analysis. He has been working with Genesis Volatility for the last three years, and currently works as a chief technical officer.

I want to thank Sascha Depold for not only being a great programmer but also a great mentor and leader. Always willing to give insightful input and a hand wherever it's needed. I want to also thank everyone who has contributed to Sequelize. It's been a great experience, and a blessing, to witness a project go from infancy to enterprise and through all of its trials and tribulations. I also want to thank the Packt team for doing an amazing job and keeping this project going during troubled times and extending deadlines and moving mountains. You guys did one heck of a great job, thank you!

About the reviewers

Sascha Depold is the original author of the first-of-its-kind Node.js ORM Sequelize. He is an experienced software engineer and engineering manager who has worked for companies such as DaWanda (now part of Etsy), Contentful, and eBay. In his spare time, he likes to collaborate with different tech schools, where he teaches software patterns and approaches as well as recent technology trends (such as GraphQL and Docker/Kubernetes). Sascha is also the creator of the platform-independent wishlist app bitte.kaufen, which makes heavy use of Sequelize under the hood.

Benjamin Coe works on the open source libraries yargs, nyc, and c8, and is a core collaborator on Node.js. He's a manager of a team at Google that generates idiomatic client libraries for eight programming languages.

Table of Contents

Part 1 – Installation, Configuration, and the Basics

1

Introduction to Sequelize and ORM in Node.js   3

2

Defining and Using Sequelize Models   35

Part 2 – Validating, Customizing, and Associating Your Data

3

Validating Models   77

4

Associating Models   97

5

Adding Hooks and Lifecycle Events to Your Models   127

6

Implementing Transactions with Sequelize   143

7

Handling Customized, JSON, and Blob Data Types   163

Part 3 – Advanced Queries, Using Adapters, and Logging Queries

8

Logging and Monitoring Your Application   177

9

Using and Creating Adapters   187

10

Deploying a Sequelize Application   211

Index   235

Other Books You May Enjoy   246

Preface

From idling on the runway to flying in the skies, this book will introduce you to the world of corresponding with a database for a Node.js application using Sequelize and MySQL, from generating a schema and fitted for an airline agency to deploying a web application for booking flights in the cloud.

Concepts such as event life cycles, associations, transactions, and pooling connections are covered to get you from start to finish when working on your next application. By the end of this book, you will be proficient and confident in creating, removing, and transforming data between a database management system and a Node.js application using Sequelize.

Who this book is for

This book is for beginner to intermediate JavaScript developers who are new to creating Node.js applications and want to attach a database to their web applications. Having SQL knowledge is a plus, but not a prerequisite, for understanding this book's contents.

What this book covers

Chapter 1, Introduction to Sequelize and ORM in Node.js, covers installing the necessary prerequisites for the book's lessons.

Chapter 2, Defining and Using Sequelize Models, covers mapping out your database schema and reading or writing to it.

Chapter 3, Validating Models, covers how to ensure the integrity of your models' data.

Chapter 4, Associating Models, will help you learn the basics and advantages of creating relationships between models.

Chapter 5, Adding Hooks and Lifecycle Events to Your Models, will go through the order of operations for life cycle events with real-world applicable examples.

Chapter 6, Implementing Transactions with Sequelize, covers encapsulating transactional queries with several different isolation and lock levels.

Chapter 7, Handling Customized, JSON, and Blob Data Types, covers using documented and miscellaneous storage in a relational database.

Chapter 8, Logging and Monitoring Your Application, helps you identify issues and bottlenecks in your application.

Chapter 9, *Using and Creating Adapters*, covers how to extend, add, and plug into the Sequelize library to create new tools and platforms.

Chapter 10, *Deploying a Sequelize Application*, covers how to deploy the Avalon Airlines project to a cloud application platform such as Heroku.

To get the most out of this book

All code examples have been tested using Node.js 16, MySQL 5.7, and Sequelize 7 on macOS and Linux. However, the code base should still work with future version releases.

Software/hardware covered in the book	Operating system requirements
Node.js 16	Windows, macOS, or Linux
MySQL 5.7	Windows, macOS, or Linux
Sequelize 7	Windows, macOS, or Linux

If you are using the digital version of this book, we advise you to type the code yourself or access the code from the book's GitHub repository (a link is available in the next section). Doing so will help you avoid any potential errors related to the copying and pasting of code.

Download the example code files

You can download the example code files for this book from GitHub at `https://github.com/PacktPublishing/Supercharging-Node.js-Application-with-Sequelize`. If there's an update to the code, it will be updated in the GitHub repository.

We also have other code bundles from our rich catalog of books and videos available at `https://github.com/PacktPublishing/`. Check them out!

Download the color images

We also provide a PDF file that has color images of the screenshots and diagrams used in this book. You can download it here: `https://packt.link/FqVKp`.

Conventions used

There are a number of text conventions used throughout this book.

`Code in text`: Indicates code words in text, database table names, folder names, filenames, file extensions, pathnames, dummy URLs, user input, and Twitter handles. Here is an example: "Mount the downloaded `WebStorm-10*.dmg` disk image file as another disk in your system."

A block of code is set as follows:

```
models.sequelize.sync({
    force: true,
    logging: false
})
```

When we wish to draw your attention to a particular part of a code block, the relevant lines or items are set in bold:

```
// INT(4)
var unsignedInteger = DataTypes.NUMBER({
    length: 4,
    zerofill: false,
    unsigned: true,
});
```

Any command-line input or output is written as follows:

```
sudo apt-get update
sudo apt install mysql-server
```

Bold: Indicates a new term, an important word, or words that you see onscreen. For instance, words in menus or dialog boxes appear in **bold**. Here is an example: "We will want to select the **Developer Default** and **Install all products** options."

> **Tips or important notes**
> Appear like this.

Get in touch

Feedback from our readers is always welcome.

General feedback: If you have questions about any aspect of this book, email us at customercare@ packtpub.com and mention the book title in the subject of your message.

Errata: Although we have taken every care to ensure the accuracy of our content, mistakes do happen. If you have found a mistake in this book, we would be grateful if you would report this to us. Please visit www.packtpub.com/support/errata and fill in the form.

Piracy: If you come across any illegal copies of our works in any form on the internet, we would be grateful if you would provide us with the location address or website name. Please contact us at copyright@packt.com with a link to the material.

If you are interested in becoming an author: If there is a topic that you have expertise in and you are interested in either writing or contributing to a book, please visit authors.packtpub.com.

Share Your Thoughts

Once you've read *Supercharging Node.js Applications with Sequelize*, we'd love to hear your thoughts! Scan the QR code below to go straight to the Amazon review page for this book and share your feedback.

https://packt.link/r/1801811555

Your review is important to us and the tech community and will help us make sure we're delivering excellent quality content.

Download a free PDF copy of this book

Thanks for purchasing this book!

Do you like to read on the go but are unable to carry your print books everywhere?

Is your eBook purchase not compatible with the device of your choice?

Don't worry, now with every Packt book you get a DRM-free PDF version of that book at no cost.

Read anywhere, any place, on any device. Search, copy, and paste code from your favorite technical books directly into your application.

The perks don't stop there, you can get exclusive access to discounts, newsletters, and great free content in your inbox daily

Follow these simple steps to get the benefits:

1. Scan the QR code or visit the link below

https://packt.link/free-ebook/9781801811552

2. Submit your proof of purchase

3. That's it! We'll send your free PDF and other benefits to your email directly

Part 1 – Installation, Configuration, and the Basics

In this part, you will learn how to install and configure Sequelize for your operating system, and how to insert, delete, update, and query data from your database.

This part comprises the following chapters:

- *Chapter 1, Introduction to Sequelize and ORM in Node.js*
- *Chapter 2, Defining and Using Sequelize Models*

1

Introduction to Sequelize and ORM in Node.js

Managing database drivers, managing schematics, maintaining a business' workflow, and validating data can be daunting for any programmer. Along with perpetually changing business requirements, organizing the business logic into database models can be cumbersome. This usually entails the programmer finding all applicable references and updating queries manually. This could be an expensive operation for both the project and the programmer; without proper testing, the modifications could result in errors within the application or erroneous logic, leaving the programmer, the business, and the customer in a state of confusion.

This book will help guide you through the process of installing, building, maintaining, upgrading, extending, querying, and applying database schematics using an **object-relational mapping** (**ORM**) framework in a Node.js application using the Node.js runtime environment. The book can be read from start to finish in a sequential manner, or if you are more experienced, you can read the chapters that interest you directly. Each chapter complements the previous chapter since we will be creating an entire application from scratch. However, more experienced programmers can skip between chapters with the understanding that there may be "gaps" within their data model and what is shown within the chapter. The concepts and methodologies taught in each chapter, regardless of your data's structure, will still be applicable.

The goal of this chapter is to help you become familiar with what Sequelize is and which capabilities are offered to you from using Sequelize. We will go over the necessary prerequisite steps for installing applicable libraries, frameworks, runtime engines, and **database management systems** (**DBMS**). By the end of this chapter, you will have acquired the knowledge and skillset of installing, configuring, and running an application, under the Node.js runtime with Sequelize, from scratch.

The first chapter of this book will cover the following topics:

- Introducing Sequelize
- Advantages of using Sequelize over other alternatives

- Installing the necessary applications, frameworks, and tools to help get you started
- Configuring Sequelize within an Express application

Technical requirements

Before we embark on our journey of developing an application with Sequelize, there are a few prerequisites. We will need to install the following:

- A DBMS such as MySQL
- The Node.js runtime library
- A few Node.js packages: Sequelize, Express, and a MySQL driver

Introducing Sequelize

Sequelize (also known as **SequelizeJS**) is an ORM framework that helps connect and correspond your Node.js application to a database. Sequelize has been in development since 2010 by Sascha Depold and is used extensively within *Fortune 100* companies. Throughout the years, the framework has grown to nearly 25,000 *stargazers* on GitHub, with over 900 contributors, and is used by over 300,000 open sourced projects. Sequelize has been *battle-tested* for performance and security for over a decade and has performed without issues for major retail stores and web agencies (such as Walmart and Bitnami) even during their highest traffic times of the year.

What started out as a master's thesis turned into a major integral building block of Node.js' ecosystem.

> **Note**
>
> An ORM is a methodology of associating database structures and information using **object-oriented (OO)** decorations and patterns. An ORM's purpose is to help alleviate the differences between DBMSs and to offer some form of abstraction for querying and manipulating data more ergonomically. Typically, an ORM will also come with helper functions to help manage the state of connections, pre-validation of data, and workflows.

The framework follows a **promise-based** approach, which allows programmers to invoke data asynchronously. The promise-based approach offers a more convenient way of managing returned values, or errors, within your application without waiting for the result(s) to return immediately. To learn more about promises and how to program with them, refer to the following link: `https://developer.mozilla.org/en-US/docs/Web/JavaScript/Reference/Global_Objects/Promise`.

What is asynchronous?

Think of asynchronous as a way to perform tasks without having to wait for a response before continuing on with another task. When you text message someone, you do not have to wait for their response in order to continue with your day. After you send a message, you usually would not warrant any attention to the correspondence until you receive a signal that there was a response or that the message had failed to send.

Currently, Sequelize supports the following DBMSs: MySQL, MariaDB, Postgres, **Microsoft SQL Server** (**MSSQL**), Snowflake, **Database 2** (**DB2**), and SQLite. An ORM offers more than just a connector to your database. ORMs often offer features such as the following:

- Tooling for migrating schemas and data
- Adapter/plugin support
- Connection pooling
- Eager loading of data
- Managed transactions

Now that we understand *what* Sequelize is and its basic capabilities, we will go over *why* we should use an ORM such as Sequelize over alternative methods such as **data access objects** (**DAOs**) or querying the database directly. Some of the advantageous capabilities include being able to handle and organize queries within transactions or migrating schematic changes to a database.

Advantages of using Sequelize over other alternatives

There are many alternative ways of querying the database from your application. There are ORMs, DAOs, raw database drivers, and so on. Each methodology has its pros and cons and caters to different programming styles and conventions. Typically, those who favor *convention over configuration* tend to gravitate toward ORMs, while those who favor configuration tend to use DAO frameworks or raw database drivers.

An ORM can handle data validation, similar to DAOs, with additional features such as reading and writing from a database using a driver. With ORMs, you would not need to manage query statements manually, which could save you time over the DAO or raw connection methods.

Note

An ORM is not mutually exclusive to DAOs. You can think of DAOs as being explicit as opposed to being implicit and presumptuous. A DAO only provides an *interface* for your data. It does not involve how/where you read or write the data (the database driver), nor will it concern itself with the data's integrity unless the application manually invokes some form of data validation outside of the DAO's scope.

When using an ORM such as Sequelize, you will have the following features without any additional code:

- Transaction handling
- Connection pooling
- Model/data validation
- Data integrity (outside of DBMS' scope of **foreign keys (FKs)**, unique constraints, and so on)
- Eager loading
- Schematic migration and cascading
- Optimistic locking

Using a DAO or a raw database driver will forfeit these features, and you will have to build these solutions yourself. Using an ORM such as Sequelize will help you build your project with more efficiency and efficacy.

So far, we have covered the *what* and *why* for Sequelize; now, we will be going over the *how* for installing the necessary prerequisites for our application.

Installing the necessary applications, frameworks, and tools to help get you started

Our application will require customers to view information from a centralized source, and we will need to capture information that they have entered into our database. Usually, customers can either view your product/services via an application that they install on their machine or they can use a browser to visit our website. Node.js is a good choice for building web applications, which is what we'll be building throughout this book, due to its **central processing unit** (**CPU**)-bound limitations and ease of context switching between *frontend development* (what is displayed to the end user) and *backend development* (what the end user does not see but still invokes) owing to Node.js being JavaScript. We will need to install the following applications/programs in order to get started:

- A DBMS (we will be installing MySQL)
- Node.js runtime
- Sequelize and Express

Installing MySQL

This next section will go over the installation process for MySQL on three different operating system distributions: Microsoft Windows, macOS, and Linux. MySQL was chosen due to the ease of installation (no need to mess with configurations or **access-control lists** (**ACLs**)). Do not let those points discourage you from using a different database. For the most part, Sequelize will be able to gracefully translate from one DBMS to another, and the majority of this book will use common/standard **Structured Query Language** (**SQL**) methods.

Windows

The MySQL installer for Microsoft Windows can be found here:

`https://dev.mysql.com/downloads/mysql/5.7.html`

> **Note**
>
> The default **Uniform Resource Locator** (**URL**) for downloading Windows' MySQL installer is currently at version 8.0.26. This book uses version 5.7, but other versions of MySQL should still work appropriately as long as the Node.js MySQL driver is compatible with that version.

Once we are finished downloading and opening the installer application, you will be greeted with the **Choosing a Setup Type** screen. We will want to select the **Developer Default** and **Install all products** options, as illustrated in the following screenshot:

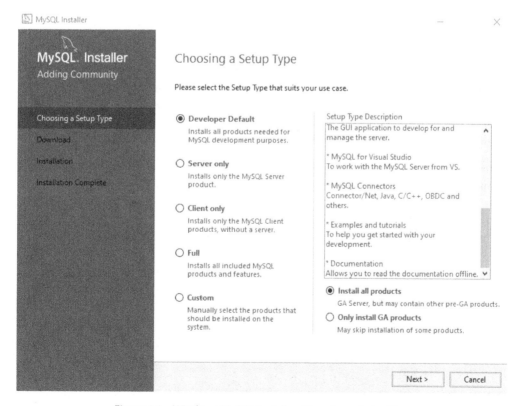

Figure 1.1 – Windows MySQL Installer: Choosing a Setup Type

If you have Python or Visual Studio installed on your computer, you may be greeted with a **Check Requirements** step (see *Figure 1.2*). If you are using Visual Studio as your **integrated development environment (IDE)**, then you may install the necessary products, but it is not a requirement. Throughout your projects, you may come across a utility that is written in Python that interacts with your database (for example, most data science-related libraries/frameworks). By selecting the **Connector/Python** option shown in the following screenshot, we can avoid potential headaches in the future:

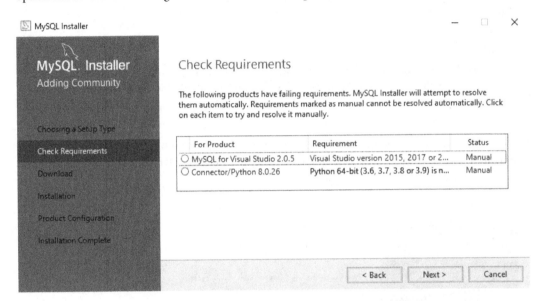

Figure 1.2 – Windows MySQL Installer: Check Requirements

The next section should be the **Download** step. The main products that we will be required for the contents of this book are listed here:

- **MySQL Server**
- **MySQL Workbench** (for a **graphical user interface (GUI)** to our database)
- **MySQL Shell**

You can see the aforementioned products in the following screenshot:

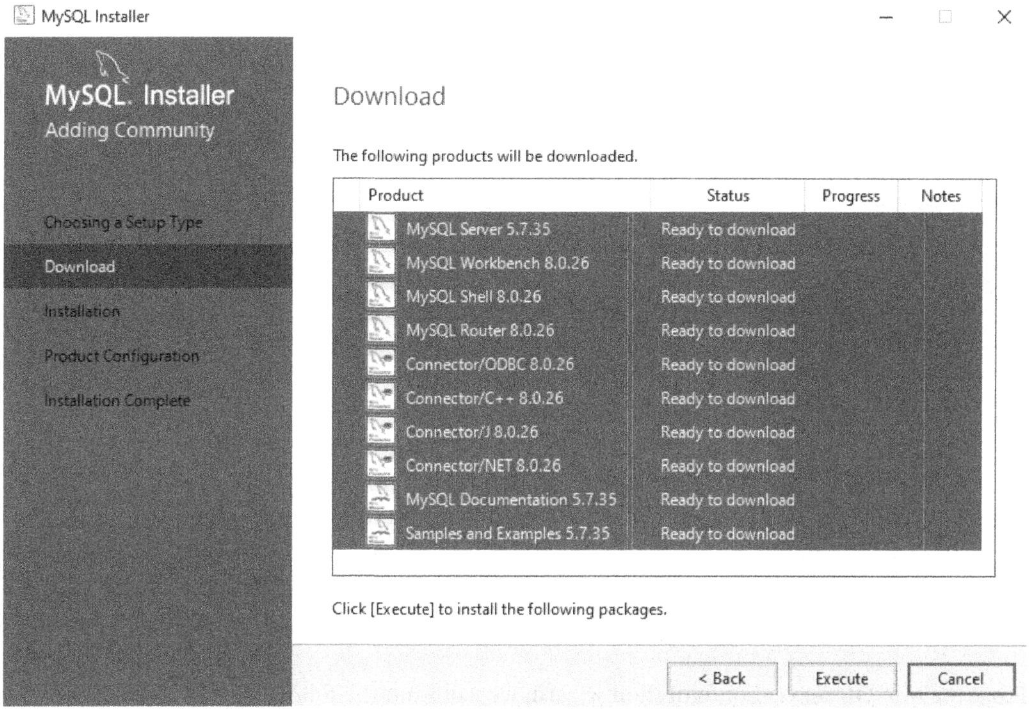

Figure 1.3 – Windows MySQL Installer: Download

> **Note**
>
> If you are new to MySQL, it may be a good idea to download the **MySQL Documentation** and **Samples and Examples** packages.

After we have finished downloading our packages, we will be entering our configuration details for each applicable selected product (for example, **MySQL Server** and **Samples and Examples**). For the majority of the configuration settings, we will be using the default values; however, there will be some steps that will require your intervention. You can see an overview of this in the following screenshot:

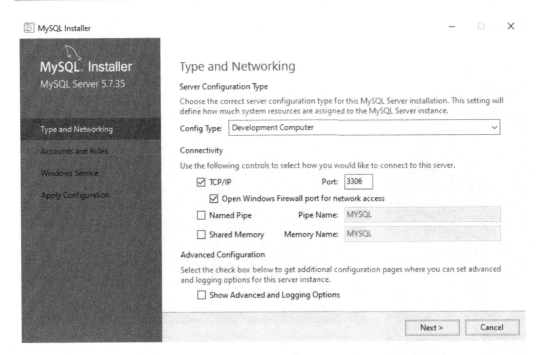

Figure 1.4 – Windows MySQL Installer: Type and Networking

From the **MySQL Server** configuration wizard, we will want the following settings (as shown in *Figure 1.4*):

- **Config Type**: **Development Computer**
- **TCP/IP**: Checked
- **Port**: 3306
- **Open Windows Firewall port for network access**: Optional

The next part of the MySQL Server configuration step is to declare your MySQL root password and user accounts. Make sure to keep this information in a safe place in case you run into administration issues throughout your projects. If you forget the MySQL root password, there are several methods for resetting the password, as explained here: `https://dev.mysql.com/doc/mysql-windows-excerpt/5.7/en/resetting-permissions-windows.html`.

For setting up a MySQL user account with a role, you will be greeted with the following **Accounts and Roles** screen:

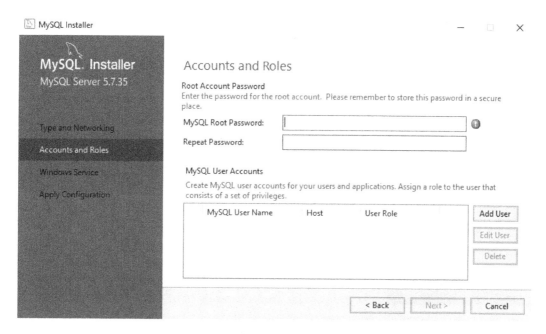

Figure 1.5 – Windows MySQL Installer: Accounts and Roles

Within the **MySQL User Accounts** section, you will need to click on the **Add User** button (near the right side of the window, as shown in *Figure 1.5*) and type in a username and password that you will memorize for when we initialize our Node.js application. When you are finished adding the appropriate root password and MySQL user account(s), we can proceed to the next step.

Next, the installation process will offer a **Configure MySQL Server as a Windows Service** option, as illustrated in the following screenshot. **Windows Service** is a **process control system** (**PCS**) that will also orchestrate background processes (in the Unix/Linux world, these are referred to as *daemons*):

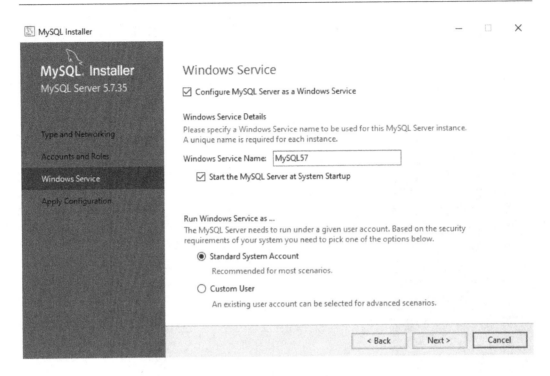

Figure 1.6 – Windows MySQL Installer: Windows Service

We will want to ensure the following parameters are configured (as shown in *Figure 1.6*):

- **Configure MySQL Server as a Windows Service**: Checked

- **Start the MySQL Server at System Startup**: Checked

- **Standard System Account** selected under the **Run Windows Service as...** section

Click on **Next >** to apply our configurations for the MySQL server. If you selected additional packages to install earlier, you may be prompted with additional screens asking for more configuration settings and parameters.

> **Note**
>
> If you selected the **MySQL Router** package from the previous section, the installation process will ask you for information on how you would like to set up a cluster environment. It is not recommended to install this package unless you are a database administrator or you are setting up a production environment. Simply uncheck the **Bootstrap MySQL Router for use with InnoDB cluster** option and click **Finish** to proceed without installing MySQL under a cluster environment.

If the **Samples and Examples** package was selected for installation, we will be prompted with a screen that will allow us to enter our MySQL username and password. You may use your *root credentials* for the username and password input fields and click on the **Next >** button to continue. An overview of the screen is provided in the following screenshot:

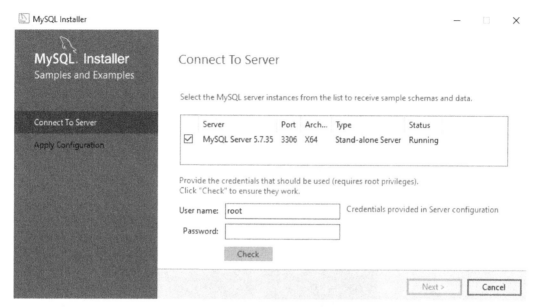

Figure 1.7 – Windows MySQL Installer: Connect To Server

macOS

There are a couple of ways to install MySQL on a macOS machine. The first way is to download and install MySQL from a **Disk iMaGe (DMG)** file, while another method is by using a package manager such as Homebrew. We will explore both options.

Installing from disk image

You can find the appropriate disk image from the following URL: `https://dev.mysql.com/downloads/mysql/` (x86 for Intel CPUs and **Advanced RISC Machine (ARM)** for M1 CPUs).

Note

If you cannot find version 5.7 for MySQL, you will find the appropriate DMG file from MySQL's archive link: `https://downloads.mysql.com/archives/community`.

However, the macOS installation packages may not be available to download for the most recent 5.7 versions. At the time of writing this book, versions 5.7.34, 5.7.33, and 5.7.32 are not available as a DMG package (5.7.31 is available to download). Any applicable 5.7 version should be compatible with this book's instructions and installation procedures.

If you are asked about installing a preference panel throughout the installation process, we recommend you do so. Otherwise, we will need to consult the **Installing a MySQL Launch Daemon** page, located at `https://dev.mysql.com/doc/refman/5.7/en/macos-installation-launchd.html`.

After downloading and opening the DMG file, we will want to open the **package (pkg)** file, which will start our installation process. Depending on your macOS version, you may be prompted with a **"[package name]" can't be opened because Apple cannot check it for malicious software** screen, as shown here:

Figure 1.8 – Apple cannot identify the package for maliciousness

If this is the case for you, go to **Apple | Security & Privacy**, and the window should have an **Open Anyway** button next to **"mysql….pkg" was blocked from use because it is not from an identified developer.**, as shown in the following screenshot:

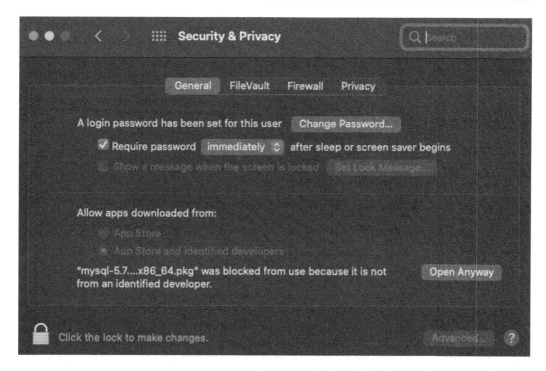

Figure 1.9 – Bypassing unidentified package installations

Once the installation package opens again, you may be prompted with another alert from Apple. Click on **Open** to continue with the installation process. After continuing and reading the **software license agreement** (**SLA**), you may select the default installation location. Clicking on **Install** may prompt for your administrative password, as illustrated in the following screenshot:

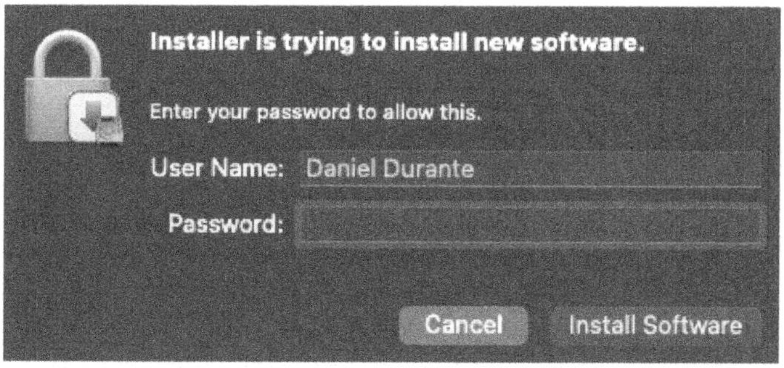

Figure 1.10 – MySQL installation asking for administrative permission

Once the MySQL installer finishes, an alert dialog will appear with a temporary password. An example is shown in the following screenshot. Make sure to take note of the temporary password for when we log in to the MySQL server:

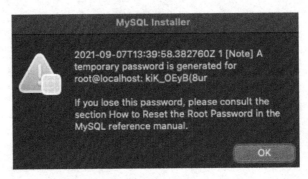

Figure 1.11 – MySQL installation providing a temporary root password

Installing from Homebrew

Using Homebrew over traditional package installers can help keep your packages up to date without manual intervention, along with validating package installations and binaries. To install MySQL through Homebrew, we will need to install Homebrew on our local machine. Within the terminal (located in **Applications** > **Utilities**), simply type in the following:

```
/bin/bash -c "$(curl -fsSL https://raw.githubusercontent.com/
Homebrew/install/HEAD/install.sh)"
```

> **Note**
> It is always a good idea to double-check an external script's contents before running commands from it. A web page can redirect to anywhere, including malicious scripts that could lead to data breaches or something more nefarious.

When installing Homebrew, you may come across the following message:

```
==> Checking for `sudo` access (which may request your
password)
```

You can see an illustration of this in the following screenshot:

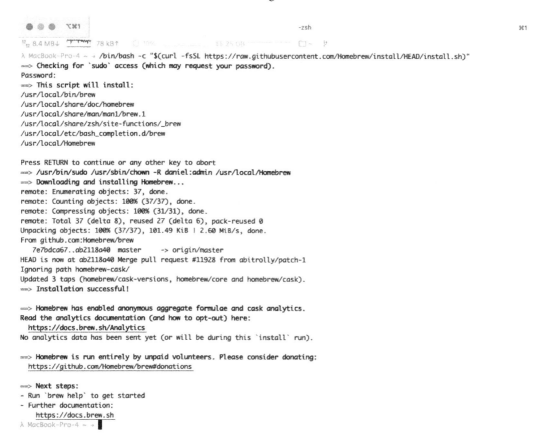

Figure 1.12 – Installing Homebrew on macOS

You can either enter in your password here or before installing Homebrew, run sudo <anything> (for example, sudo ls), enter in your password, and then run the installation command. The user must have administrator access before continuing.

For this book, we will install MySQL version 5.7. Other versions of MySQL should be compatible with the book's code base, as previously noted. To install version 5.7 explicitly, run the following command:

```
brew install mysql@5.7
```

There may be additional steps and commands to run in order to set up your instance properly, as illustrated in the following screenshot. The book's contents will not require library/header files for compilation, nor for pkg-config to be configured. As a general rule, it is recommended to run mysql_secure_installation and go through the prompts for adding a root password, but it is not a requirement:

Figure 1.13 – Installing MySQL with Homebrew on macOS

Next, we will need a way to manage our MySQL service. There are two options available to us, as outlined here:

- Manually create launch daemon configuration files. More information on how this can be achieved is available here: https://dev.mysql.com/doc/refman/5.7/en/macos-installation-launchd.html.

- We can use a Homebrew extension known as services to manage launch configurations automatically by executing the following command:

```
brew tap homebrew/services
```

In order to start the MySQL service, we need to run the following command:

```
brew services start mysql@5.7
```

If you prefer a GUI version of managing your services, there is an application called `brew-services-menubar` that can be installed via Homebrew's Cask extension, as shown in the following code snippet:

```
brew install --cask brewservicesmenubar
```

> **Note**
>
> If you prefer to use a GUI when interfacing/querying databases, there is a free application called Sequel Pro that is available for downloading here:
>
> `http://www.sequelpro.com/`

Linux

There are numerous distributions of Linux; for this book, we will be using Ubuntu (any Debian distribution should be applicable with the same commands). If you are using a different distribution, please refer to this page for instructions on how to install MySQL for your operating system: `https://dev.mysql.com/doc/refman/5.7/en/linux-installation.html`.

Within the terminal, run the following commands (these are also shown in the screenshot that follows):

```
sudo apt-get update
sudo apt install mysql-server
```

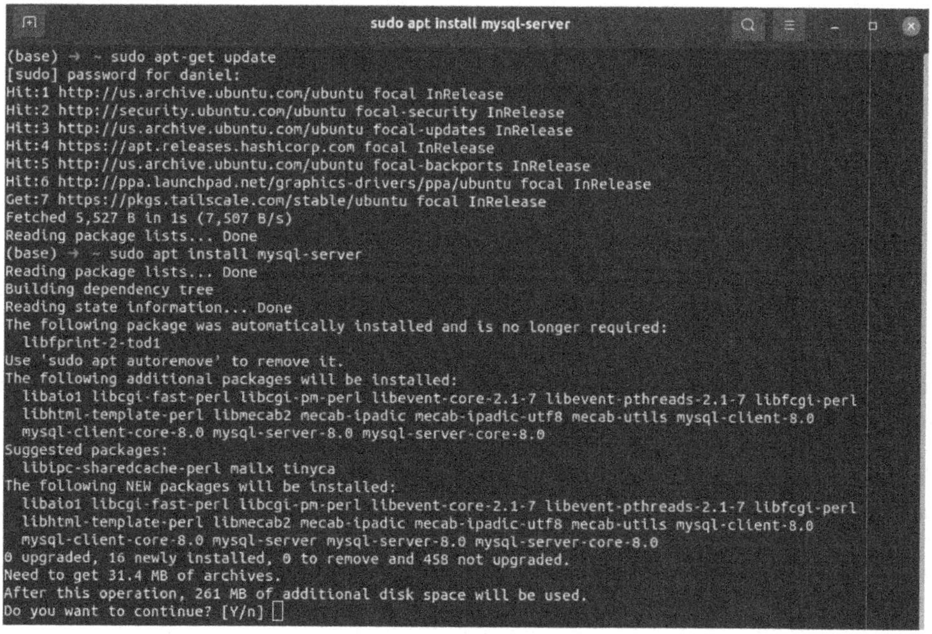

Figure 1.14 – Installing MySQL Server on Ubuntu

After MySQL has finished its installation, we will need to initialize a database to store all of our model's schemas and information. Some ORMs and DBMSs will refer to databases as "schemas" (not to be confused with a model's schema, which is referred to as "attributes" in Sequelize specifically).

Creating a database

Now that we have finished installing the MySQL DBMS engine on our local machine, we can start creating a database with some tables. Before creating tables, we will need to go over the various types of MySQL engines. Luckily for us, the following is applicable to all operating systems in the same way.

By default, MySQL will create an InnoDB database type (or, in MySQL terms, engine). Database engines are associated with the database's table on MySQL (and not the entire database itself). This is useful when you know the trade-offs between a read-heavy table with no constraints (for example, news articles) and a write-heavy table (for example, a chatroom). For the sake of brevity, we will go over the main three database engines, as follows:

- **InnoDB**: A database engine with transactional queries and FK support. Transactional queries are useful for executing a query, or several queries, with atomicity. We will go into further details about transactions and FKs in a later chapter.

- **MyISAM**: If the majority of your database's operations are read-related and you do not require any data constraints, this would be a preferred database engine to use.

- **HEAP**: The data stored within these tables is contained within the machine's memory. This database engine is useful if you had to query against temporary data quickly. MySQL will not manage memory allocations for you, so it is important to remember to delete tables when they are no longer in use (and that the data fits into the machine's available memory).

> **Note**
> You can always check your local MySQL server's default engine type by entering the following command within a MySQL client: SELECT @@default_storage_engine;.

You may skip this section and use the Sequelize **command-line interface**'s (**CLI**'s) (installation instructions are given later within this chapter) db:create command, as long as the applicable MySQL user has the appropriate permissions. For the intent of becoming familiar with the terminal, we will create the database using command lines, as shown in the next screenshot.

Log in to the MySQL server with the following command (you may be prompted to enter in a password, or the additional -p parameter is required to enter in a password):

```
mysql --user=root
```

We can create our database by executing the following SQL command within the MySQL client Command Prompt:

```
CREATE DATABASE airline;
```

> **For Windows users**
>
> Most of these commands are executable via the Command Prompt or PowerShell applications. These applications can be accessed from the **Start** menu (for example, **Start** > **All Programs** > **Accessories** > **Windows PowerShell**).

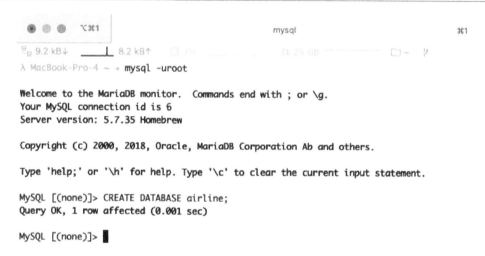

Figure 1.15 – Creating a database

If you are using a Windows machine, you may use any terminal application of your choice (Command Prompt, PowerShell, and so on), or you can use MySQL Workbench, as shown in the following screenshot, which we installed in the previous section:

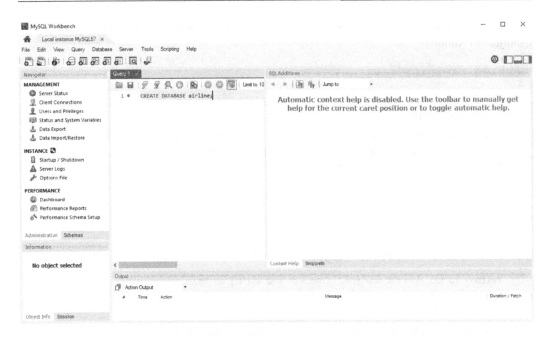

Figure 1.16 – MySQL Workbench: Creating a database

> **Note**
>
> To execute a query using MySQL Workbench, there is a *thunderbolt* icon within the query's toolbar (the icon is usually next to the *save* icon). Your query's results will appear at the bottom of your screen in the **Output** section.

Installing Node.js

At the time of writing this book, the **long-term support** (**LTS**) version of Node.js is 16. Throughout this book, we will be using this version of Node.js, but the code base should still execute without issues using other releases. All of the corresponding operating system installations of Node.js can be found here: `https://nodejs.org/en/download/`.

> **Note**
>
> If the LTS version of Node.js is no longer version 16 and you want to use the same version as this book, you can download previous Node.js versions here: `https://nodejs.org/en/download/releases/`.
>
> For managing multiple Node.js versions on one machine, there is an application called **Node Version Manager** (**NVM**) that can handle and maintain several versions of Node.js on the same machine. For more information, you can visit their repository at `https://github.com/nvm-sh/nvm`.

Windows

After we are done downloading and opening the Node.js Windows installer, we will be prompted with the following screen:

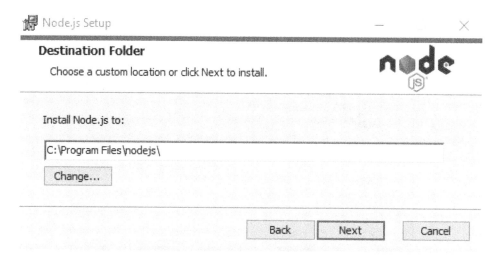

Figure 1.17 – Windows Node.js installer: Destination Folder

Clicking on **Next** will bring us to the **Custom Setup** step of the installation. Ensure that you are installing/configuring the following:

- **Node.js runtime**
- **npm package manager**
- **Add to PATH**

You can see an overview of this screen here:

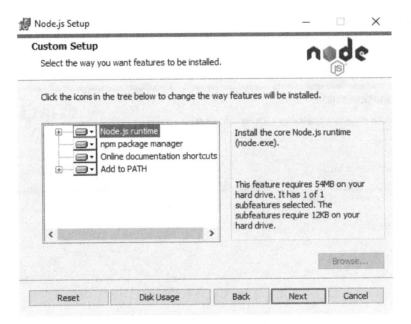

Figure 1.18 – Windows Node.js installer: Custom Setup

After the **Custom Setup** step, we will be brought to a **Tools for Native Modules** section. By default, the checkbox for installing the necessary tools is unchecked. For development purposes, we will want to make sure that the automatic installation option is checked, as depicted in the following screenshot:

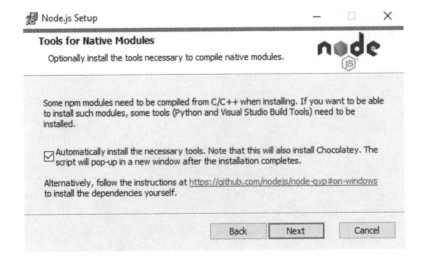

Figure 1.19 – Windows Node.js installer: Tools for Native Modules

Selecting the automatic tool installation will prompt a PowerShell window to appear, as illustrated in the next screenshot, showing you the status of installation progress for Chocolatey, .NET packages, Python dependencies, and so on.

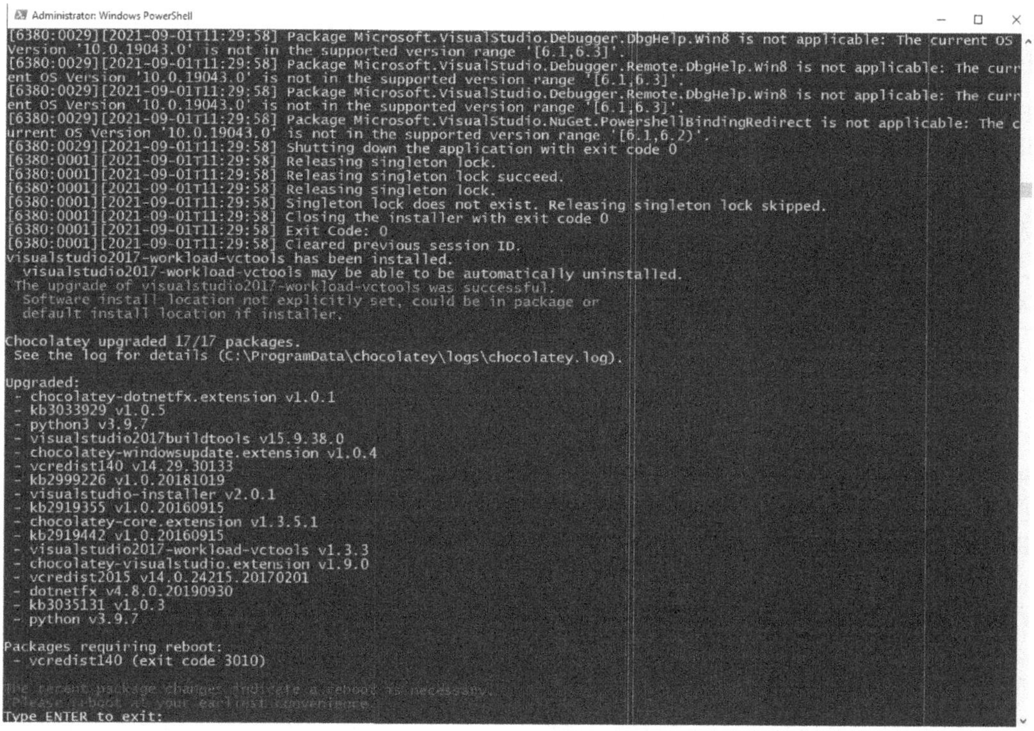

Figure 1.20 – Windows Node.js installation: additional tools

> **Note**
>
> Chocolatey is a package manager for Microsoft's Windows operating system. If you are familiar with the macOS environment, this would be similar to Homebrew or Apt on a Debian Linux distribution. For more information on Chocolatey, please refer to the following link: `https://chocolatey.org/`.

macOS

You can install Node.js for macOS via its package image, which is located at `https://nodejs.org/en/download/`, or you can install it with Homebrew by running the following command:

```
brew install node@16
```

To confirm that your machine is using the correct "node" binary, we can always check the version by running the following command:

```
node -v
```

Linux

For Ubuntu/Debian Linux distributions, we can use a specific repository to install Node.js 14, as illustrated in the following code snippet:

```
sudo apt update
curl -sL https://deb.nodesource.com/setup_14.x | sudo bash -
```

After the repository has been added, we can install Node.js and check the version, like so:

```
sudo apt -y install nodejs
node -v
```

So far, we have finished installing MySQL as our DBMS, applicable package managers, and the Node.js runtime library; we can now begin to scaffold our project and install the necessary Node.js packages for Sequelize and Express.

Configuring Sequelize within an Express application

After we have installed our development tools and database, we can begin installing and configuring our application with Sequelize and **Express**. Express is a minimal web framework for Node.js runtime applications. Our Node.js application will use Sequelize to correspond with the database, and Express will relay those query results to the browser. More information on Express, along with a complete reference, can be found here: https://expressjs.com.

Within Command Prompt, PowerShell, or the terminal, enter the following commands for initializing our project:

```
mkdir airline
cd airline
npm init -y
```

This will create a directory called `airline`; then, we will change our working directory to the `airline` folder, and we will run an initialization script from the **node package manager** (**npm**). The npm command will create a `package.json` file that contains a bare configuration for npm to use on this project. After that, we will need to install the minimum required Node.js modules for our application, as follows:

```
npm install express @sequelize/core mysql2
```

Here is an online resource that you may refer to for a complete list of options for npm:

`https://docs.npmjs.com/cli/v7/commands`

Sequelize has a companion executable to help us initialize our project, manage updates to our schema, and handle database migrations. We can install it as a global (`--location=global`) binary within our userspace by entering the following command in our terminal:

```
npm install --location=global sequelize-cli
```

For a full list of commands available to you, the CLI has documentation built in that can be exposed using the `-h` or `--help` flags, as illustrated in the following screenshot:

Figure 1.21 – Sequelize CLI installation and help guide

The next step is to initialize a generic template that Sequelize provides for us from the CLI. This will generate several directories for configuration, migration, seed, and model files. Here's the code to do this:

```
sequelize init
```

The following list offers a brief explanation of the directories created by the CLI in our project's directory:

- `config`: A directory that contains a database connection configuration file in **JavaScript Object Notation (JSON)** format. The `sequelize-cli` tool uses this configuration file to migrate schema and data files, but these configuration settings could also be used for our Node.js application as well.

- `migrations`: A directory containing Node.js files with instructions for Sequelize on how to scaffold your database's schema and structure.

- `models`: A collection of Node.js files with Sequelize schema definitions.

- `seeders`: Similar to the `migrations` directory but instead of defining our database's schema, we will define our database's data.

Now that we have the initial foundation of our application, we can edit our Sequelize configuration file located in `config/config.json`. Depending on which installation instructions you followed, the username and password values may be different than the book's code base. The code is illustrated in the following snippet:

```
{
  "development": {
    "username": "root",
    "password": null,
    "database": "airline",
    "host": "127.0.0.1",
    "dialect": "mysql"
  },
  "test": {
    "username": "root",
    "password": null,
    "database": "airline",
    "host": "127.0.0.1",
    "dialect": "mysql"
  },
  "production": {
    "username": "root",
```

```
      "password": null,
      "database": "airline",
      "host": "127.0.0.1",
      "dialect": "mysql"
    }
  }
```

If you do not wish to keep usernames and passwords in a file (which is a good idea for production environments or version control repositories), there is an alternative form for the configuration file that can accept an environment key with a connection **Uniform Resource Identifier (URI)** resource as the input (for example, `mysql://root:password@127.0.0.1:3306/airline`), as illustrated in the following code snippet:

```
{
  "development": {
    "use_env_variable": "DB_DEV_ENV"
  },
  "test": {
    "use_env_variable": "DB_TEST_ENV"
  },
  "production": {
    "use_env_variable": "DB_PRODUCTION_ENV"
  }
}
```

If we wanted to use the `development` configuration, our Node.js application would know to look for the connection parameters/URI from an environment variable called DB_DEV_ENV (you may use the same environment variable for any stage). For more options and configuration settings for the Sequelize CLI, refer to this resource: `https://github.com/sequelize/cli/blob/master/docs/README.md`.

> **Note**
>
> You can toggle between which environment you would like your application to be in by setting a NODE_ENV environment variable. The default value is `development` but if we wanted to use our `production` environment, we would set the environment like so: NODE_ENV=`production`.

Connecting Sequelize with Express

We can now begin building our Node.js application by creating an `index.js` file within the project's directory and opening the file in our IDE of choice. Let us begin by typing in the following code:

```
const express = require("express");
const app = express();


const models = require("./models");

models.sequelize.sync().then(function () {
    console.log("> database has been synced");
    }).catch(function (err) {
    console.log(" > there was an issue synchronizing the
                    database", err);
});

app.get('/', function (req, res) {
    res.send("Welcome to Avalon Airlines!");
});

app.listen(3000, function () {
    console.log("> express server has started");
});
```

We begin by declaring our Express/web application variables (`express` and `app`) with the first two lines of the code. The next line is shorthand for invoking the `./models/index.js` file that was created by the Sequelize CLI from earlier (we will go into details of that file in the next chapter). The following line runs the Sequelize `sync()` command, which will synchronize your model definitions with a database by creating the necessary tables, indices, and so on. It will also establish associations/relations, execute sync-related hooks/events, and so on.

The `sync()` command offers several options that are encapsulated within an object as the first parameter, as outlined here:

- `force`: A Boolean value that will drop your database's tables before re-creating them.

- `match`: A **regular expression** (**regex**) value to match against table names to sync. Useful for testing or to ensure only certain tables are affected by the `force` option within a production environment.

- `logging`: A Boolean or function value. `true` (the default) will use `console.log` when executing queries for logging. `false` will disable entirely, and a function can be used to send logs and context to another adapter. This book will go into detail about this option in a later chapter.

- `schema`: A string value for defining which database to operate in. Useful for when you are using a DBMS such as Postgres, which allows you to separate tables by not only a database (which MySQL calls a "schema") but also by a namespace (which Postgres calls "schema").

- `searchPath`: A string value to define the default `search_path` for Postgres databases only. This option will not pertain to this book's code base or content.

- `hooks`: A Boolean value (defaults to `true`) to execute several hooks/events that are related to sync events (`beforeSync`, `afterSync`, `beforeBulkSync`, and `afterBulkSync`). `false` will disable events from executing.

- `alter`: An object with the following parameter:

  - `drop`: A Boolean value that prevents any `drop` statements from being executed when Sequelize needs to run `ALTER` commands within the database.

You can define these options like so:

```
models.sequelize.sync({
   force: true,
   logging: false
})
```

> **Note**
>
> It is *not* recommended by the Sequelize community to run the `force` option as `true` within a production environment. This could have unintentional consequences such as deleting vital customer/user information. The `force` option is for when you are still prototyping your application and want to start your application on a clean slate per iteration.

The next command, `app.get(...)`, instructs the Express framework to route the `"/"` (root) path of our web application to the scoped function (in this case, we are sending text back to the browser, as shown in *Figure 1.22*). After that, we start the Express server by calling `app.listen(...)`, which will tell our application to listen for **Hypertext Transfer Protocol** (**HTTP**) events on port `3000`, which can be accessed in our browser via `http://localhost:3000` or `http://127.0.0.1:3000`, depending on your network interface settings. For starting our application, we can run the following command within our terminal/PowerShell:

```
node index.js
```

You should see text displayed on your screen indicating the following:

- Express has started

- A SQL query was executed

- The database has been synced

> **Note**
>
> Sequelize will automatically execute a SELECT 1+1 AS result query as a method for checking on the database connection's health. Not all DBMSs offer a way of sending a ping packet to check whether a connection is successful or not.

Now, when you open your browser and visit the previously mentioned URL, you should see a page similar to what is shown here:

Figure 1.22 – Welcome page

Every time we make a change to our application, we will need to terminate our current process (*Ctrl + C*) within the terminal. This will send a SIGINT signal to the process, which will send an interrupt signal to the process in order to begin cleaning up and then exit/stop. To avoid having to restart our process manually after every change, we can install a separate process to help facilitate this for us called Nodemon (more information can be found here: https://nodemon.io/).

Nodemon may be installed as a global binary by running the following command:

```
npm install -g nodemon
```

You can confirm if the installation was successful by typing in the following:

```
nodemon index.js
```

This should start our Node.js application while simultaneously watching for changed files within our project's directory. Once we have made a modification to the project, we should see Nodemon automatically restarting our process, as illustrated in the following screenshot:

Figure 1.23 – Nodemon automatically restarting the application

The last step for this chapter is to make a few adjustments to our `package.json` file, as follows:

- Add `"private": true` under the `"name": "airline,"` line. This adjustment will prevent us (or anyone else on the team) from publishing our project to the public npm registry.

- Look for the `scripts` object and replace whatever content is there with `"start": "nodemon index.js"`. This will allow us to start our application by running the following command:

  npm run start

The final `package.json` file should look similar to this:

```
{
  "name": "airline",
  "private": true,
  "version": "1.0.0",
  "description": "",
  "main": "index.js",
  "scripts": {
    "start": "nodemon index.js"
  },
  "author": "",
  "license": "ISC",
  "dependencies": {
```

```
        "express": "^4.17.1",
        "mysql2": "^2.3.0",
        "@sequelize/core": „latest"
    }
}
```

Summary

In this chapter, we introduced the benefits of using an ORM and what Sequelize has to offer. We learned how to set up our development/local environment to run a DBMS (MySQL) and the Node.js runtime. We then scaffolded a project using npm and the Sequelize CLI and integrated the Sequelize library with the Express web framework.

In the next chapter, we will begin inserting data into our database and define Sequelize models.

2
Defining and Using Sequelize Models

For our *Avalon Airlines* project that we introduced in the previous chapter, we will need to instruct our application on how we want to define our database's schematics. A database can have various roles and applications but only a single purpose, and that purpose is to organize our data (storage is the filesystem's job). Before we can begin defining our models within the Node.js application, we need to think about the entities of our business logic and models from a project's perspective (and each project will have different requirements). Most projects will structure their schema in a way that categorizes *organizations* (for example, customers, employees, vendors, and companies) and *things* such as products, planes, and receipts from transactions.

Object-relational mapping (ORM) helps us ensure that the database is organized from the data and team's perspective. Sequelize will help us manage the nomenclature for our project (for example, whether to define tables using a `snake_case` or with a `PascalCase` pattern). Relations—or associations—between models will be automatically created and managed by Sequelize. Business logic workflows can also be established so that you do not have to remember workflows such as *removing the customer's boarding pass if they canceled their trip*. That part would be handled in one organized place versus invoking `RemoveBoardingPass(...)` in every code section that cancels a trip (regardless of whether the method was called from the customer, an employee, and so on). This chapter will teach you how to define and synchronize your models with a database and how to apply the data to a Node.js runtime application using Sequelize. This will be the initial foundation on how to operate Sequelize.

This chapter will introduce you to the following concepts:

- Defining models for a database
- Exploring the various Sequelize data types and when to use them
- Migrating schematic changes and data from Sequelize to the database
- Manipulating and querying data using Sequelize
- Advanced Sequelize options for defining models

Technical requirements

You can find the code files present in this chapter on GitHub at `https://github.com/PacktPublishing/Supercharging-Node.js-Applications-with-Sequelize/tree/main/ch2`

Defining models for a database

In this section, we will go over a brief overview of our project's requirements and establish which kinds of models we need to define. After that, we will run a script generator command from the Sequelize **command-line interface (CLI)** tool and inspect the basic structure of a model's definition.

For *Avalon Airlines*, we will begin modeling with the following *organizations* and *things*:

- Airplanes
- Customers
- Flight schedules
- Boarding tickets

Each model will have its own table within the database. We will eventually associate these models or tables with columns, indices, validation, and relations to other models. For now, we will define, select (or query), insert, update, and delete data from these tables using Sequelize within our Node.js application. If you are working on a pre-existing project that already has a database, the *Manipulating and querying data using Sequelize* section will pertain to you more than to someone starting on a project from a clean slate.

We will first generate our models with the minimum requirements for columns using the Sequelize CLI tool. Then, we will go over the code that was generated by the CLI so that you are more familiar with how to define Sequelize models without depending on the CLI. Generate the previously mentioned models with the following commands within the project's root directory:

```
sequelize model:generate --name Airplane --attributes
planeModel:string,totalSeats:integer

sequelize model:generate --name Customer --attributes
name:string,email:string

sequelize model:generate --name FlightSchedule --attributes
originAirport:string,destinationAirport:string,
departureTime:date

sequelize model:generate --name BoardingTicket --attributes
seat:string
```

You may have noticed we used a singular noun for our models' names. Sequelize will automatically pluralize the associated table and models for us. You can disable this behavior via Sequelize configuration settings, which will be discussed in detail further in this chapter. For our `BoardingTickets` model, we will generate associations of a customer and flight schedules in the next chapter, but for now, we can build the bare minimum for the table.

> **Tip**
>
> Sequelize comes with some useful utility functions available to the developer. The framework uses a library called **Inflection**, which comes with a set of string manipulation functions. Sequelize exposes underscore, singularize, and pluralize functions directly from `Sequelize`.

Opening the `models/flightschedule.js` file, we should see the following generated code:

```
'use strict';
const {
  Model
} = require('@sequelize/core');
module.exports = (sequelize, DataTypes) => {
  class FlightSchedule extends Model {
    /**
     * Helper method for defining associations.
     * This method is not a part of Sequelize lifecycle.
     * The `models/index` file will call this method
       automatically.
     */
    static associate(models) {
      // define association here
    }
  };
  FlightSchedule.init({
    originAirport: DataTypes.STRING,
    destinationAirport: DataTypes.STRING,
    departureTime: DataTypes.DATE
  }, {
    sequelize,
    modelName: 'FlightSchedule',
```

```
  });
  return FlightSchedule;
};
```

The `'use strict';` line in the preceding code snippet will tell our Node.js runtime to execute the JavaScript file (`models/flightschedule.js`) with a set of rules to help alleviate **sloppy mode**. **Strict mode** will prohibit the developer from assigning values to undeclared variables, using reserved keywords as defined by **ECMAScript 2015 (ES6)**, and so on. This mode is completely optional for the contents of this book; however, if you wish to learn more, Mozilla offers a helpful guide on the differences between strict and sloppy mode here: `https://developer.mozilla.org/en-US/docs/Web/JavaScript/Reference/Strict_mode/Transitioning_to_strict_mode`.

The next set of instructions is to import the `Model` class from Sequelize, which we will use to initialize the model in the next few commands. The `module.exports` line that follows is a pattern that the Sequelize model loader (the `models/index.js` file) can interpret and how to invoke the file. The first argument provides an instance of Sequelize to us with all of the parameters and configuration settings that we established from the `models/index.js` file. The second parameter, `DataTypes`, provides a more ergonomic way of declaring the various data types for our columns (for example, instead of having to type out `sequelize.DataTypes.STRING`, we can omit the `sequelize.` instance prefix and just use `DataTypes.STRING`).

Next, we define our `FlightSchedule` class and extend Sequelize's `Model` class. Here, we can define our associations, hooks/events, table information, and so on. The CLI will generate a static function for us called **associations**. For now, we can leave this function as is; we will modify it later throughout the book.

The last instruction within this file takes our `FlightSchedule` class and invokes the `init()` function, which will set up internal rules and instructions to help Sequelize navigate the model's definition. This is also where Sequelize learns how to synchronize the model with the database, as shown in the following screenshot. If you were to set Sequelize's option to `sync: true`, there would be additional **Structured Query Language (SQL)** commands executed such as `DROP TABLE IF EXISTS` for when we want to test our application on a clean slate every runtime. Having the sync option set to `true` is useful for unit tests and early prototype development. It is *not* recommended to set this option to `true` within a production environment:

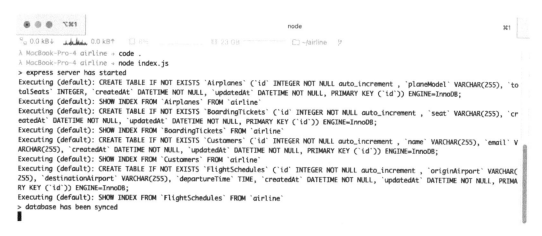

Figure 2.1 – Sequelize's automatic synchronization

> **Note**
>
> Running our Node.js application and letting Sequelize synchronize our database is fine for the initial implementation phase, but we will go over the methodology of using Sequelize's CLI and migrations to perform the necessary SQL commands to synchronize the database. Migrations offer incremental changes/updates as opposed to the Sequelize synchronize option, which is more of a generic solution.

The first parameter of the init() function is where we define our model's attributes (or columns). The pattern for this is typically an object with the keys as column names and the value for each key is either a DataType, a literal string value, or an object containing advanced options for each column. From this example, we are shown three columns (originAirport, destinationAirport, and departureTime) with string, string, and date data types respectively.

The second parameter lets us define instance type settings for the model explicitly. This is where we can define a different table name, choose whether to pluralize our tables, disable meta columns (such as createdAt and updatedAt), and so on. We will go into details about these options later in this chapter.

If you prefer to not use classes in your project, there is another way to define our models. The following code snippet provides an example of using Sequelize's define() function:

```
module.exports = (sequelize, DataTypes) => {
    return sequelize.define('FlightSchedule', {
        originAirport: DataTypes.STRING,
        destinationAirport: DataTypes.STRING,
        departureTime: DataTypes.DATE
```

```
    }, {
        sequelize,
    });
  };
```

The parameters remain relatively the same as `init()` except that the first parameter is now the model's name. Either way is acceptable and one does not provide advantages over the other from Sequelize's point of view. This book will use the former example throughout its code base (the `Model` class), but for advanced configuration settings and adding associations, this book will illustrate both styles as there are some fundamental differences, ergonomically speaking. For programmers who favor using TypeScript over JavaScript, the `Model` class method may provide a more native experience to you.

Now that we have an understanding of how models are defined in Sequelize, we can go over which built-in attribute data types Sequelize has to offer, along with a brief explanation to help guide your future model designs.

Exploring the various Sequelize data types and when to use them

As explained earlier, Sequelize offers us various data types to help map our model's attributes to their respective **database management system** (**DBMS**) column types. Next is a list of what Sequelize has to offer, along with a brief explanation.

STRING

The `STRING` data type refers to a **Variable Character Field** (**VARCHAR**) column type, which is a non-fixed character column. The maximum storage for this column type varies depending on the DBMS. `VARCHAR` fields usually contain meta information to help optimize the DBMS' query planner. MySQL explicitly adds another byte to the column's prefix header if the size of the string is greater than 255 bytes. A query planner could use this information to help alleviate pressure from memory, or the **central processing unit** (**CPU**), when retrieving/collecting/analyzing the data. To call `VARCHAR` with a fixed paging length, you would define the column as `DataTypes.STRING(100)` instead of `DataTypes.STRING`.

Within a `VARCHAR` column type, the DBMS will not store the value as a fixed length (no padding is required). If you need data to be retrieved in the exact same way it was stored, you could use the `VARCHAR BINARY` column type. This can be achieved by declaring the column's data type as `DataTypes.STRING.BINARY`.

Despite having the word "binary" in the data type's name, for storing movies, pictures, and so on, it is often recommended to use the `BLOB` type over `VARCHAR BINARY`. The binary part of `VARCHAR BINARY` performs comparisons over the binary representation of that column versus a **character set** (**charset**).

For instance, suppose we had the following rows in a database: A, a, B, and b. The VARCHAR column type would have an internal map to tell the database that "A" and "a" will be listed prior to "B" and "b". In a VARCHAR BINARY column, the sum binary representation of A, a, B, and b would be 0, 2, 1, 3, which would sort into the following: A, B, a, b. There is no internal map/charset for VARCHAR BINARY columns, so the database would not be able to tell that "A" and "a" are actually the same letter.

For the most part, we could use VARCHAR BINARY and BLOB interchangeably in MySQL versions above 5.0.2. There are some small subtle differences, as indicated here:

- An index prefix length must be specified for BLOB indexes
- BLOB column types cannot have default values

CHAR

The CHAR data type is similar to the STRING data type, except that it references the CHAR column type. Traditionally, a DBMS will cap the length of a CHAR column to 255 characters. A VARCHAR type will allow you to go over the specified paging size without an error or an exception. A CHAR column could be used as a last-resort effort for validating your data and ensuring it does not exceed the specified length (for example, CHAR(20) would cap the data to 20 characters defined by the table's collation). CHAR column types are padded to their fixed length, which could help optimize the DBMS—or even your application—presuming that the pre-determined length is appropriate for the scenario's paging size.

TEXT/TINYTEXT/MEDIUMTEXT/LONGTEXT

Database designers understand that sometimes, our text data requires a considerable amount of space or needs to be associated with rows larger than 65,535 bytes (a MySQL VARCHAR limitation). In this case, we would use a TEXT column type. Every DBMS has its nuances and limitations; since this book uses MySQL, we will briefly go over MySQL's TEXT limitations, as follows:

- TINYTEXT: 255 bytes
- TEXT: 64 **kilobytes (KB)**
- MEDIUMTEXT: 16 **megabytes (MB)**
- LONGTEXT: 4 **gigabytes (GB)**

DataTypes.TEXT will default to the TEXT column type, and if you wanted to declare your column type as TINYTEXT, MEDIUMTEXT, or LONGTEXT, you would use DataTypes.TEXT('TINY'), DataTypes.TEXT('MEDIUM'), or DataTypes.TEXT('LONG'), respectively. Unlike the VARCHAR type, there is no BINARY option for TEXT column types. For storing serialized binary types, you would use VARCHAR BINARY or BLOB instead.

CITEXT

CITEXT stands for **Case-Insensitive Text**, which is a column that preserves the data's casing except for comparison operations. This option is available for Postgres and SQLite databases only.

NUMBER

Not to be confused with Postgres' NUMERIC type, the NUMBER data type is an abstraction for more than an explicit type, depending on its configuration settings. This data type should *not* be used directly unless you are extending/adding your own numeric data type. This abstract data type could help organize your code if you use the same precision and scale values throughout your database, or if your online store sells a product in different denominations and currencies.

The following code snippet provides an example of how you would extend your own numeric data type:

```
// INT(4)
var unsignedInteger = DataTypes.NUMBER({
    length: 4,
    zerofill: false,
    unsigned: true,
});


// FLOAT(5,4)
var specificFloat = DataTypes.NUMBER({
    length: 5,
    zerofill: false,
    unsigned: false,
    decimals: 4
});

// DECIMAL(6,4)
var specificPrecision = DataTypes.NUMBER({
    zerofill: false,
    unsigned: false,
    precision: 6,
    scale: 4
});
```

INTEGER/TINYINT/SMALLINT/MEDIUMINT/BIGINT

With `DataTypes.INTEGER`, `DataTypes.SMALLINT`, and so on, we can associate our attributes with the respective column types. You can find references for minimum and maximum values for each integer type with MySQL here: `https://dev.mysql.com/doc/refman/5.7/en/integer-types.html`. To declare your model's attribute as an unsigned value, we can attach the `UNSIGNED` option to our data type, like so:

```
DataTypes.INTEGER(21).UNSIGNED
```

If we wanted to have our attribute unsigned and zero-filled, we can chain the data-type options, as follows:

```
DataTypes.INTEGER(21).UNSIGNED.ZEROFILL
```

> **Note**
>
> Depending on which DBMS you use, the `ZEROFILL` option may not be available to you. If you are using a Postgres database, then the order of assigning those attributes is important (`UNSIGNED` must be declared before `ZEROFILL`). In MySQL, the `ZEROFILL` option will also imply `UNSIGNED` automatically. The `ZEROFILL` attribute will only affect the data from an aesthetics perspective (when you select data) and will not modify your data in storage.

FLOAT/REAL

Traditionally, a DBMS will differentiate between `FLOAT` and `REAL` column types by their bit precisions. `FLOAT` columns are usually stored with 32-bit precision, and `REAL` column types are stored with 64-bit precision. **Microsoft SQL Server (MSSQL)** is the inverse of this, where `REAL` column types are 64-bit and `FLOAT` columns are 32-bit. To make things even more confusing, MySQL will treat `REAL` as the same as a `DOUBLE` (also known as `DOUBLE PRECISION` and `DECIMAL`) column.

Internally, Sequelize handles `FLOAT`, `REAL`, and `DOUBLE` in the same way. There is a small float validation performed for the `FLOAT` type explicitly, but otherwise, Sequelize will translate the column type directly to the DBMS. Just as with the integer data types, `UNSIGNED` and `ZEROFILL` can be defined on these attributes as well, as follows:

```
DataTypes.FLOAT.UNSIGNED.ZEROFILL
```

DECIMAL/DOUBLE

The DECIMAL or DOUBLE data type allows us to define a precise length and scale for our columns using the traditional format of DECIMAL(P, S) where P > S. The P variable is the number's precision and the S variable is the number's scale. The precision determines the maximal length of the whole number part, and the scale defines the maximal length of the decimal part. For example, DataTypes.DECIMAL(6, 4) will give us a decimal column with a precision of 6 and a scale of 4. An example value for this column could be 38.3411.

> **Note**
> You may use DataTypes.NUMERIC as an alias for DataTypes.DECIMAL.

BOOLEAN

There are many ways to express a **Boolean**. Some applications prefer to use numerical values (or as a single bit) of 0 for false and 1 for true. Sometimes, the Boolean value will be stored as a string such as true, false, t, or f. Sequelize will automatically handle numerical—or bit—values, as well as the "true" or "false" string expressions as appropriate Boolean values for Node.js. If the value is marked as "t" or "f", then Sequelize will pass the raw value along to the programmer to handle (as a way to avoid being over presumptuous—this behavior may change in the future). A Boolean column can be defined with just DataTypes.BOOLEAN. There are no arguments or inputs to process for this data type.

DATE/DATEONLY/TIME

The DATE data type references the DATETIME column types for MySQL, MariaDB, and SQLite. For Postgres, the DATE data type will be translated as TIMESTAMP WITH TIME ZONE.

In MySQL, you can define fractional seconds for DATETIME columns by up to six digits, like so:

```
DataTypes.DATE(6)
```

If you wish to keep just the date or time, you may use DataTypes.DATEONLY or DataTypes.TIME, respectively.

Quick note on Postgres without time zones

If you are using Postgres with a column type of TIMESTAMP WITHOUT TIME ZONE, and you know the data's time differentiates that from the server that is running the application, it is recommended to set the time zone's offset. This can be achieved via the pg Node.js library, as illustrated here:

```
var types = require('pg').types
function setTimestampWithoutTimezoneOffset(val) {
    // '+0000' being the UTC offset, change this to the desired
time zone
    return val === null ? null : new Date(stringValue + '+0000');
}
types.setTypeParser(types.builtins.TIMESTAMP,
setTimestampWithoutTimezoneOffset);
```

For more information on setting types for Postgres within Node.js, refer to the following link: https://github.com/brianc/node-pg-types

NOW

DataTypes.NOW is a special type within Sequelize. It is not to be used as the column's type but as the attribute's value and is traditionally set as the attribute's defaultValue option. If we wanted a Receipt model that kept track of when a transaction was made, it would look similar to this:

```
Receipt.init({
    total: DataTypes.DECIMAL(10,2),
    tax: DataTypes.DECIMAL(10,2),
    dateOfPurchase: {
        type: DataTypes.DATE,
        defaultValue: DataTypes.NOW
    }
}, {
    sequelize,
    modelName: 'Receipt'
});
```

Whenever we insert a Receipt record, Sequelize will automatically convert the dateOfPurchase attribute's value to the DBMS' NOW() function from the attribute's defaultValue option using Sequelize's DataTypes.NOW data type. If we have defined a value for the attribute initially, then Sequelize will use that value instead.

HSTORE

HSTORE is for Postgres only. This data type is used for mapped key-value types but is often replaced by JSON or **JSON Binary** (**JSONB**). If your project requires the use of HSTORE, there is a caveat to keep in mind, which is to install the pg-hstore Node.js library. The full installation command would look like this:

```
npm install --save sequelize pg pg-hstore
```

For selecting data, in Sequelize, your where clause would be an object instead of an integer, string, and so on. An example would look like this:

```
MyModel.find({
  where: {
    myHstoreColumn: {
      someFieldKey: 'value',
    }
  }
});
```

JSON

The JSON data type is available for SQLite, MariaDB, MySQL, and Postgres. When defining an attribute with the JSON type, you can query information similar to how the HSTORE type is queried, with the exception of having the ability to deeply nest your search clause. Let us say we had the following JSON data type stored in a column:

```
{
    "someKey": {
        "deeply": {
            "nested": true
        }
    }
}
```

We would search for the nested value like so:

```
MyModel.find({
    where: {
        myJsonColumn: {
            someKey: { deeply: { nested: true } }
```

```
        }
    }
});
```

Please note that MySQL and MariaDB introduced support for **JavaScript Object Notation (JSON)** fields in MySQL 5.7.8 and MariaDB 10.2.7 respectively. For former versions, you can define models with situations where the `DataTypes.JSON` attribute type will not be compatible with your database. To resolve this issue, you can define models with getters/setters that will store and retrieve the JSON document, like so:

```
sequelize.define('MyModel', {
    myJsonColumn: {
        type: DataTypes.TEXT,
        get: function () {
            return JSON.parse(this.getDataValue('value'));
        },
        set: function (val) {
            this.setDataValue('value',JSON.stringify(val));
        }
    }
});
```

> **Note**
>
> For users of MSSQL 2016 and above, please refer to `https://sequelize.org/master/manual/other-data-types.html#mssql` as a workaround for handling JSON column types with this DBMS.

JSONB

The `JSONB` data type is reserved for Postgres only. If you are using a JSON column for storage, it is recommended to use the `JSON` column type, and if you are using comparison operators on the column, it is recommended to use the `JSONB` column type.

Other than the previously mentioned way of querying JSON data, you can also query JSONB data types with the following formats:

```
// String matching
MyModel.find({
  where: {
    "someKey.deeply.nested": {
```

```
      [Op.eq]: true
    }
  }
});

// Using the Op.contains operator
MyModel.find({
  where: {
    someKey: {
      [Op.contains]: {
        deeply: {
          nested: true
        }
      }
    }
  }
});
```

BLOB

Several databases, including MySQL, offer a range of **binary large object** (**BLOB**) types. Regardless of the input for the BLOB attribute type, Postgres will always be converted into a bytea (byte array) column type. This data type is useful for storing anything binary-related, such as images, documents, or serialized data. You can see an example of it in use here:

```
DataTypes.BLOB // BLOB
DataTypes.BLOB('tiny') // TINYBLOB
DataTypes.BLOB('medium') // MEDIUMBLOB
DataTypes.BLOB('long') // LONGBLOB
```

Here is a table of different BLOB types with their byte prefix length and their maximum storage length for MySQL:

BLOB Type	Byte Prefix Length	Maximum Storage (in bytes)
TINYBLOB	1 byte	$2^8 - 1$
BLOB	2 bytes	$2^{16} - 1$
MEDIUMBLOB	3 bytes	$2^{24} - 1$
LONGBLOB	4 bytes	$2^{32} - 1$

RANGE

RANGE data types are reserved for Postgres only. Supported range types are INTEGER, BIGINT, DATE, DATEONLY, and DECIMAL. You may define an attribute with the range type like so:

```
var MyModel = sequelize.define('MyModel', {
    myRangeColumn: DataTypes.RANGE(DataTypes.INTEGER)
});
```

There are a couple of ways to create ranges for our models, as illustrated here:

```
// inclusive boundaries are the default for Sequelize
    var inclusiveRange = [10, 20];


MyModel.create({ myRangeColumn: inclusiveRange });

// inclusion may be toggled with a parameter
    var range = [
      { value: 10, inclusive: false },
      { value: 20, inclusive: true }
];


MyModel.create({ myRangeColumn: range });
```

When querying a range column, the data for that attribute will always return in object notation with the value and inclusive keys.

UUID/UUIDV1/UUIDV4

A **universally unique identifier** (**UUID**) is a 128-bit label with some sort of constraints and stipulations for uniqueness and near to no chance of a collision with other values. The UUIDV1/ UUIDV4 data types work in conjunction with the UUID attribute type. We can declare a model that has a default UUIDV4 value as its **primary key** (**PK**) like so:

```
sequelize.define('MyModel', {
    id: {
        type: DataTypes.UUID,
        defaultValue: DataTypes.UUIDV4,
        allowNull: false,
        primaryKey: true
    }
});
```

VIRTUAL

The VIRTUAL attribute type is a special type that will hydrate the data within Sequelize but will not populate the data into the database. The VIRTUAL field could be used for organizing code, validations, and extending Sequelize to any protocol or framework that requires nested typing (for example, GraphQL, **Protocol Buffers** (**Protobuf**), and so on), which is covered in *Chapter 9, Using and Creating Adapters*.

We can define a VIRTUAL attribute like so:

```
sequelize.define('MyModel', {
    envelope: DataTypes.STRING,
    message: {
        type: DataTypes.VIRTUAL,
        set: function(val) {
            // the following line is optional
            // but required if you wish to use the
               validation associated with the attribute
            this.setDataValue('message', val);
            this.setDataValue('envelope',
                              encryptTheMessage(val));
        },
        validate: {
            noDadJokes: function(val) {
                if (val === "knock knock") {
                    throw new Error("Who is there? Not this
                                    message")
                }
            }
        }
    }
});
```

For retrieving VIRTUAL attributes, we would need to define a data type as a parameter for the DataTypes.VIRTUAL invocation. If we want to pass through other attributes within our VIRTUAL attribute, we would define a list as the second parameter. An example is shown here:

```
sequelize.define('MyModel', {
    envelope: DataTypes.STRING,
    message: {
```

```
    type: DataTypes.VIRTUAL(DataTypes.STRING, ['en
    velope']),
    get: function() {
        return decryptTheMessage(this.get('envelope'));
    },
    set: function(val) {
        this.setDataValue('envelope',
                            encryptTheMessage(val));
    }
  }
});
```

ENUM

Sequelize has a `DataTypes.ENUM` attribute type for enumerated columns. At the moment, only Postgres has this feature enabled. A solution for other database engines would be to define a custom validation rule for your model that performs some sort of inclusion operator. Custom validations for our models will be discussed in the next chapter. There are three different ways of defining enumerated attributes, as illustrated here:

```
// Defining enums with function arguments
DataTypes.ENUM('a', 'b')

// Defining enums with an array argument
DataTypes.ENUM(['a', 'b'])

// Defining enums with an object argument
DataTypes.ENUM({
    values: ['a', 'b']
})
```

ARRAY

ARRAY attribute types are supported for Postgres only at the moment. This type requires a parameter of an applicable data type. You can see an example here:

```
DataTypes.ARRAY(DataTypes.STRING) // text[]
DataTypes.ARRAY(DataTypes.DECIMAL) // double precision[]
```

GEOMETRY

Sequelize can handle geometric data for MariaDB, MySQL, and Postgres (as long as the PostGIS extension is enabled). The **GeoJSON** specification (`https://tools.ietf.org/html/rfc7946`) can be useful for querying geometric data for an airline business. For example, we can mark the coordinates of an airport and the current location of an airplane to determine the estimated time of arrival without manually memorizing the Haversine algorithm (a formula to determine the distance between two points on a sphere). Reference examples can be found in the following code snippet:

```
var MyModel = sequelize.define('MyModel', {
    point: DataTypes.GEOMETRY('POINT'),
    polygon: DataTypes.GEOMETRY('POLYGON')
});

var point = {
    type: 'Point',
    coordinates: [44.386815, -82.755759]
}

var polygon = { type: 'Polygon', coordinates: [
    [
        [100.0, 0.0], [101.0, 0.0], [101.0, 1.0],
        [100.0, 1.0], [100.0, 0.0]
    ]
]};

await MyModel.create({ point, polygon });
```

In the preceding snippet, we first define our model with two attributes (`point` and `polygon`) with the respective geometry data types (for a complete list, you may reference the **Request for Comments** (**RFC**) manual previously mentioned). Then, we create our geometric objects with a set of defined values (a point will accept two coordinates, and a polygon can accept N coordinates). The last line will create an entry with the defined values for the corresponding attribute.

> **Note**
>
> GeoJSON is handled differently depending on whether we are using the Postgres or MariaDB/MySQL dialect. The Postgres dialect will call the `ST_GeomFromGeoJSON` function for interpretation of GeoJSON, and MariaDB/MySQL will use the `GeomFromText` function. The following reference goes into detail on spatial columns with MySQL: `https://dev.mysql.com/doc/refman/5.7/en/spatial-types.html`.

GEOGRAPHY

For MariaDB/MySQL, the GEOGRAPHY attribute type will work the same as the GEOMETRY type, but for Postgres, Sequelize will utilize PostGIS' geography data type. The GEOGRAPHY attribute type follows the same GeoJSON syntax as the GEOMETRY type.

> **Note**
>
> If you are looking for a complete set of utility functions and querying complex relationships between several coordinates, then the GEOMETRY type is recommended over the GEOGRAPHY type. If you need to use geodetic measurements instead of Cartesian measurements, or if you have simpler relationships over large areas, then the GEOGRAPHY type would be more applicable to you.

CIDR/INET/MACADDR

These three attribute types are for Postgres only. All of these types perform some type of internal validation respective to the type. These types do not have an input parameter. The following are brief explanations, with references, for each of these data types:

- CIDR—This stands for **Classless Inter-Domain Routing** and is used for allocating **Internet Protocol (IP)** addresses and route tables (https://datatracker.ietf.org/doc/html/rfc4632)

- INET—Common ways of identifying over the net (https://datatracker.ietf.org/doc/html/rfc6991)

- MACADDR—**Unique identifiers (UIDs)** for network interfaces (https://www.rfc-editor.org/rfc/rfc7042.html)

TSVECTOR

The TSVECTOR data type is used for searching through text columns with advanced operators available in Postgres' to_tsquery() function. These operators include wildcard matching, negate matching, and Boolean search. This attribute type is for Postgres only and will only accept string variables for values. When querying a TSVECTOR attribute, Sequelize will not interpret the attribute type with its associated functions implicitly (for example, to_tsvector). Let's suppose we have the following model definition:

```
var MyModel = sequelize.define('MyModel', {
    col: DataTypes.TSVECTOR
});
```

```
MyModel.create({
    col: 'The quick brown fox jumps over the lazy dog'
});
```

Then, we want to query a value on the col field, like so:

```
MyModel.find({
    where: { col: 'fox' }
});
```

The generated SQL would look similar to this:

```
SELECT * FROM MyModel WHERE col = 'fox';
```

Sequelize will interpret this query with an equals operator for the where clause. In order to take advantage of the TSVECTOR column type, we would have to be explicit with our intentions, like so:

```
MyModel.find({
    where: {
        col: {
            [Op.match]: sequelize.fn('to_tsvector', 'fox')
        }
    }
});
```

This will convert the where clause's operator from equal to matching (@@). The sequelize.fn method allows you to explicitly invoke a function from your DBMS. The query generated by this procedure would look like this:

```
SELECT * FROM MyModel WHERE col @@ to_tsvector('fox');
```

After learning how to define our model and which data types are available to us in Sequelize, we can now begin migrating our definitions to an actual database. Sequelize offers a migration subcommand within its command-line tool, to make this easy for us.

Migrating schematic changes and data from Sequelize to the database

We have defined our database's schema with the generated files from the command-line tool, and we are now ready to migrate those definitions to our DBMS. Using Sequelize's migrations can help teams of developers maintain the same schema structure across multiple machines. Migrations can provide a historical reference as to how your database has changed over time, which can also help us undo certain changes and revert our database's schema to a specific time.

Migrating schematic changes

The Sequelize CLI provides a convenient way of propagating updates toward a database. All of our schematic changes will be located within the `migrations` directory, and all of our data seeds will be located within the `seeders` directory. This chapter will cover only the initialization of the database's structure. In subsequent chapters, there will be examples of adding and removing columns (or indices) using the migration tool.

In the *Defining models for a database* section, we used the Sequelize CLI to generate our models, which should have created several files in the `migrations` directory. Each file is prefixed with a timestamp, a **call to action** (**CTA**) (for example, `create`), and the model's name. An example for one of the files (`20210914153156-create-airplane.js`) would look like this:

```
'use strict';
module.exports = {
  up: async (queryInterface, Sequelize) => {
    await queryInterface.createTable('Airplanes', {
      id: {
        allowNull: false,
        autoIncrement: true,
        primaryKey: true,
        type: Sequelize.INTEGER
      },
      planeModel: {
        type: Sequelize.STRING
      },
      totalSeats: {
        type: Sequelize.INTEGER
      },
      createdAt: {
        allowNull: false,
        type: Sequelize.DATE
      },
      updatedAt: {
        allowNull: false,
        type: Sequelize.DATE
```

```
      }
    });
  },
  down: async (queryInterface, Sequelize) => {
    await queryInterface.dropTable('Airplanes');
  }
};
```

Sequelize will use the scope of the up (...) method when we invoke the `migrations` subcommand. The down (...) method is reserved for when we decide to undo, or revert, a migration. The **query interface** is a database-agnostic adapter that executes generic SQL commands that are available to all supported database engines. We will go into detail about the query interface in a later chapter.

You may have noticed that Sequelize has added several columns to our model's definition. With the default settings, Sequelize will generate three additional columns, as follows:

- id—A PK as an integer value with `autoIncrement` set to `true`. The `autoIncrement` flag will create a sequence value (some databases, such as MySQL, will call sequences *auto-increment* columns).

- createdAt—This field will generate a timestamp upon the row's creation. Since this is a Sequelize-recognized column, the default value for this column does not require us to explicitly state `DataTypes.NOW` or any equivalent value. Sequelize will hydrate the row's value automatically when using applicable methods such as `create()`.

- updatedAt—Similar to the `createdAt` field, except this value will update automatically from Sequelize every time the row is updated.

> **Note**
> We can prevent Sequelize from creating these attributes automatically through configuration settings. These settings will be explained in detail later in this chapter.

In the root directory of our project, run the following command to initialize migrations:

```
sequelize db:migrate
```

This command will perform several more instructions than iterating through the `migrations` directory. Sequelize will first look for a table called `SequelizeMeta` that holds meta information on which files have already been processed through the `migrations` subcommand. After the table has been found or created, Sequelize will iterate through the `migrations` table in sequential order of the file's name (timestamps are a convenient way of maintaining this order) and skip any files found within the `SequelizeMeta` table.

> **Note**
>
> The `sequelize-cli db:migrate` and `db:seed` commands will use the `NODE_ENV` environmental variable to determine where to migrate/initialize data to. As an alternative, you can state which database to connect to with the `--url` option, like so: `sequelize db:migrate --url 'mysql://user:password@host.com/database'`.

If we made a mistake on a model's definition, after migration, we always have the option to revert our changes, like so:

```
sequelize db:migrate:undo
```

This will revert the last migration performed by Sequelize. If we want to undo all of our changes, there is another subcommand, shown here:

```
sequelize db:migrate:undo:all
```

If we want to revert all of our migrations up until a certain point (this is why prefixing your filenames with a timestamp is important for congruity), we can run the following command:

```
sequelize db:migrate:undo:all --to XXXXXXXXXXXXX-airlines.js
```

After the migration is completed, we should run the following commands:

```
$ mysql -uroot airline
mysql> show tables;
```

The tables shown in the following screenshot should be displayed:

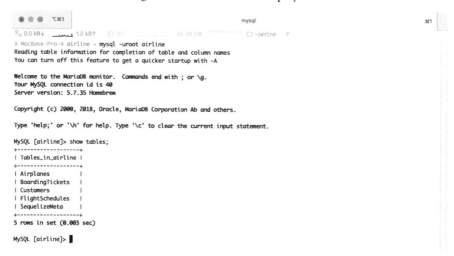

Figure 2.2 – Display of the project's tables

Initializing seed data

Now that we have our schema in place, we can start populating our database with actual data by generating seeder files within the `seeders` directory. Seed data is conventionally used for initial configuration data, static information, and so on. Good thing too—our business partner just notified us that they have purchased five airplanes to help get us started. We can create seed data for these airplanes, like so:

```
sequelize seed:generate --name initial-airplanes
```

This will generate a file in our project's `seeders` directory that contains the bare minimum for migrating seed data into the database. Similar to our migration files, there are only two methods exposed to the CLI: `up (...)` and `down (...)`.

We will replace the file's contents with the following code:

```
'use strict';

module.exports = {
  up: async (queryInterface, Sequelize) => {
    await queryInterface.bulkInsert('Airplanes', [{
      planeModel: 'Airbus A220-100',
      totalSeats: 110,
      createdAt: new Date(),
      updatedAt: new Date()
    }, {
      planeModel: 'Airbus A220-300',
      totalSeats: 110,
      createdAt: new Date(),
      updatedAt: new Date()
    }, {
      planeModel: 'Airbus A 318',
      totalSeats: 115,
      createdAt: new Date(),
      updatedAt: new Date()
    }, {
      planeModel: 'Boeing 707-100',
      totalSeats: 100,
      createdAt: new Date(),
      updatedAt: new Date()
```

```
    }, {
      planeModel: 'Boeing 737-100',
      totalSeats: 85,
      createdAt: new Date(),
      updatedAt: new Date()
    }], {});
  },

  down: async (queryInterface, Sequelize) => {
    await queryInterface.bulkDelete('Airplanes', null, {});
  }
};
```

> **Note**
>
> Unlike Sequelize's `create()` function, the query interface's `bulkInsert()` method will not hydrate the `createdAt` or `updatedAt` columns automatically. If you omit these columns from the seed file, the database will return an error since the columns do not have a default value.

Now, we can process our seed data via the following command:

```
sequelize db:seed:all
```

We can confirm the changes by entering the following SQL command into our database:

```
SELECT * FROM airplanes;
```

We then get the following results:

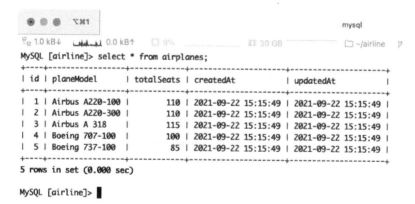

Figure 2.3 – Querying a list of airplanes

Reverting seed data is similar to the `migrations` subcommand, as we can see here:

```
sequelize db:seed:undo
sequelize db:seed:undo:all
sequelize db:seed:undo --seed <the name of your seed file>
```

> **Tip**
> Sequelize uses another project internally for migrations called Umzug. A full reference, and more examples on how to tune your migration cycle, can be found at the project's GitHub repository: `https://github.com/sequelize/umzug`.

Once we are done inserting seed data into a database, we can now query or manipulate that data using Sequelize. The following section will provide a very brief introduction for incorporating Sequelize for an Express application following more of a reference style for Sequelize. This will help give you an idea of how we will apply Sequelize in subsequent chapters for our airline project, and enough technical knowledge to help you become comfortable with making your own adjustments.

Manipulating and querying data using Sequelize

After initializing our database's structure and data, we should be able to view, modify, and remove the airplanes from our dashboard. For now, we will create very naive and simple implementations for our administrative tasks, but since we are the only technical employee at *Avalon Airlines*, this will not be a problem. As we continue creating the project, we will modify our application to become more robust and function with safety measures in mind.

Reading data

Replace the `app.get('/', ...)` block with the following code (in `index.js`):

```
app.get('/', async function (req, res) {
    const airplanes = await models.Airplane.findAll();
    res.send("<pre>" + JSON.stringify(airplanes, undefined,
            4) + "</pre>");
});
```

After that, save the file and run our application with the following command:

```
npm run start
```

Now, we can visit our website at `http://localhost:3000` and should see results similar to those shown here:

```
[
    {
        "id": 1,
        "planeModel": "Airbus A220-100",
        "totalSeats": 110,
        "createdAt": "2021-09-22T15:15:49.000Z",
        "updatedAt": "2021-09-22T15:15:49.000Z"
    },
    {
        "id": 2,
        "planeModel": "Airbus A220-300",
        "totalSeats": 110,
        "createdAt": "2021-09-22T15:15:49.000Z",
        "updatedAt": "2021-09-22T15:15:49.000Z"
    },
    {
        "id": 3,
        "planeModel": "Airbus A 318",
        "totalSeats": 115,
        "createdAt": "2021-09-22T15:15:49.000Z",
        "updatedAt": "2021-09-22T15:15:49.000Z"
    },
    {
        "id": 4,
        "planeModel": "Boeing 707-100",
        "totalSeats": 100,
        "createdAt": "2021-09-22T15:15:49.000Z",
        "updatedAt": "2021-09-22T15:15:49.000Z"
    },
    {
        "id": 5,
        "planeModel": "Boeing 737-100",
        "totalSeats": 85,
        "createdAt": "2021-09-22T15:15:49.000Z",
        "updatedAt": "2021-09-22T15:15:49.000Z"
    }
]
```

Figure 2.4 – Listing our airplanes

Now, we will create another route that will return the results to us for a specific airplane. If the airplane cannot be found, then we should send a *Not Found* **Hypertext Transfer Protocol** (**HTTP**) response code (which is 404). Add the following route below the root **Uniform Resource Locator** (**URL**) route (the app.get('/', …) block):

```
app.get('/airplanes/:id', async function (req, res) {
    var airplane = await models.Airplane.findByPk
                (req.params.id);
```

```
if (!airplane) {
    return res.sendStatus(404);
}

res.send("<pre>" + JSON.stringify(airplane, undefined,
        4) + "</pre>");
});
```

The findByPk method will try to find a record from the model's PK attribute (by default, this will be Sequelize's generated id column). When a record is found (for example, http://localhost:3000/airplanes/1), the application will return the record to us, but if we changed the id parameter from 1 to 10 (http://localhost:3000/airplanes/10), we should receive a *Not Found* response.

Here is a list with a brief explanation of Sequelize functions relating to retrieving data:

- findAll—Use this when you want to use the where clause in your query and retrieve more than one row.

- findOne—Similar to the findAll function, except that this function will return a single row.

- findByPk—A function that returns a single row using the model's defined PK.

- findOrCreate—This function will return a single instance of the row that was either found or instantiated from the database. Sequelize will compose the attributes defined within the where and defaults key.

Complex querying

Sometimes, you will need more than just a simple where clause with an AND operator. Sequelize has several operators built in to help write queries with a more complex where clause. A full list of these operators is shown here:

- and/or—Logical AND and logical OR. These values contain an array of where clause objects.

- eq/ne—Equal (=) or Not Equal (!=).

- gte/gt—Greater-Than-or-Equal (>=) and Greater-Than (>).

- lte/lt—Lesser-Than-or-Equal (<=) and Lesser-Than (<).

- is/not—IS NULL and IS NOT TRUE, respectively.

- in/notIn—IN and NOT IN operators of any array with values.

- any/all/values—ANY (Postgres only), ALL, and VALUES operators respectively.

- `col`—Converts column string values into **identifiers** (**IDs**) specified by the database/dialect.
- `placeholder`—Internal operator used by Sequelize.
- `join`—Used internally by Sequelize.
- `match`—Match operator used for text searching (Postgres only).
- `like/notLike`—`LIKE` and `NOT LIKE`, respectively.
- `iLike/notILike`—Case-insensitive version of `LIKE` and `NOT LIKE` (Postgres only).
- `startsWith/endsWith`—Shorthand for the `LIKE '%...'` and `LIKE '...%'` expressions.
- `substring`—Shorthand expression for `LIKE '%...%'`.
- `regexp/notRegexp`—`REGEXP` and `NOT REGEXP` for MySQL and Postgres only.
- `between/notBetween`—`BETWEEN x AND y` and `NOT BETWEEN x AND y`.
- `overlap`—Postgres-only range operator for overlap (`&&`).
- `contains/contained`—Postgres-only range operator for `@>` and `<@`, respectively.
- `Adjacent`—Postgres-only range operator for adjacent querying (`- | -`).
- `strictLeft/strictRight`—Strict operators for Postgres ranges (`<<` and `>>`).
- `noExtendRight/noExtendLeft`—No extension range operators for Postgres (`&<` and `&>`).

Querying a complex `where` clause may look something like this:

```
const { Op } = require("@sequelize/core");

MyModel.findAll({
    where: {
        [Op.or]: [
            { status: 'active' },
            sequelize.where(sequelize.fn('lower', se
            quelize.col('name')), {
                [Op.eq]: 'bob'
            },
            {
                [Op.and]: {
                    age: {
                        [Op.gte]: 40
                    },
                    name: {
```

```
                          [Op.like]: 'mary%'
                       }
                   }
               }
           }]
       }
   });
```

This will then produce the following query:

```
SELECT
    ...
FROM "MyModel"
WHERE (
    status = 'active'
    OR
    lower(name) = 'bob'
    OR (
        age >= 40
        AND
        name LIKE 'mary%'
    )
)
```

Deleting data

For deleting an instance (a single record), we can call a destroy() function, like so:

```
var record = MyModel.findOne({ where: { /* ... */ } });
await record.destroy();
```

> **Note**
> If there is no attribute marked as a PK within your model's definition, then Sequelize may not delete the correct record. The instance's destroy() method would be called with a where clause that tried to match all of the instance's attributes. This could lead to unintentional deletions.

To delete multiple rows at once, execute the following code:

```
MyModel.destroy({ where: { name: 'Bob' }});
```

You can remove all of a table's data by passing a configuration option to the destroy() method, like so:

```
await MyModel.destroy({ truncate: true });
// or
await MyModel.truncate();
```

Updating and saving data

Sequelize offers a few ways of updating attributes/data, depending on where you are updating from. If you wish to update multiple rows, we could use the model's update() function, like so:

```
await MyModel.update({ name: "John" }, {
  where: { name: null }
});
```

This query will update all of the records' names to John, where the current value is NULL. For updating a specific instance, we would change the attribute's value and then call the save() function, as follows:

```
var record = MyModel.findOne();
record.name = "John";
await record.save();
```

If you are in the middle of changing a record's attributes and your workflow requires you to reset the record's data back to the original values (without touching the database), you may do so with the reload() method, as follows:

```
var record = MyModel.findOne({ where: { name: 'John' } });
record.name = "Bob";
record.reload();
// the record.name attribute's value is now back to John
```

Creating data

To create a single row, the code for Sequelize would look similar to this:

```
await MyModel.create({ firstName: 'Bob' }, { ... });
```

The second parameter accepts the following options for create():

- raw—If this Boolean value is set to true, then Sequelize will ignore the **virtual setter attributes** within the model's definition. This is useful when you want to skip transforming the data through setter functions and wish to use the raw values that are provided from the query directly instead.

- isNewRecord—A Boolean value that can enable (if set to true) Sequelize's behavior for applying default values, updating a timestamp column, and so on. The default value for this method is true.

- include—An array containing include options for Sequelize. This book will provide examples and further details in a later chapter.

- fields—An array of strings containing column names that will filter which attributes will be updated, validated, and saved.

- silent—If this value is set to true, then Sequelize will not update the updatedAt timestamp column.

- validate—A Boolean value to toggle whether or not to execute validations.

- hooks—A Boolean value that enables/disables running before/after create, update, and validate life cycle events.

- logging—A function that will pass down the query's statement.

- benchmark—Logs execution query time (in milliseconds) and will be passed as the second parameter for the logging function.

- transaction—You may pass a transaction Sequelize instance for this option.

- searchPath—Postgres-only option for defining which search_path to use when querying.

- returning—Postgres-only option for selecting which fields to return when creating a new record. A Boolean true value will return all of the fields, but an array of strings will filter which columns to return.

Bulk-inserting data is very similar to creating a single row with Sequelize. The following code snippet illustrates an example of this:

```
await MyModel.bulkCreate([
    { firstName: 'Bob' },
    { firstName: 'William' }
], {...});
```

The first parameter is an array of values, and the second parameter is for configuration options. These options are identical to the `create()` method: `fields`, `validate`, `hooks`, `transaction`, `logging`, `benchmark`, `returning`, and `searchPath`. In addition, the `bulkCreate()` method also offers us the following options:

- `individualHooks`—Executed before/after create life cycle events for each record individually. This does not affect bulk before/after life cycle events.

- `ignoreDuplicates`—Ignores duplicated rows by any constrained key defined on the table. This feature is not supported on MSSQL or Postgres versions below 9.5.

- `k`—An array of fields to update if there is a duplicated key entry (for MySQL/MariaDB, SQLite 3.24.0+, and Postgres 9.5+ only).

Ordering and grouping

When sifting through your data, you can order (or group) your columns like so:

```
MyModel.findAll({
    where: { name: 'Bob' },
    order: [
        ['name', 'DESC']
    ]
});
```

For grouping, depending on which database you are using, you may have different results from other database engines (such as requiring you to select only aggregated functions and grouped columns). Consult your database's documentation for the specific nuances and rules that are required for grouping. Here is an example of a simple GROUP BY statement:

```
MyModel.findAll({ group: 'name' });
```

> **Caution**
>
> Sequelize will treat the group's input as a literal value. If you are grouping by user-generated content, it is highly recommended to escape your value to avoid SQL injections (`https://en.wikipedia.org/wiki/SQL_injection`). You may escape values using the `sequelize.escape('...');` method.

Limits and pagination

We can simply use the `offset` and `limit` key values for our finder methods, like so:

```
MyModel.findAll({ offset: 5, limit: 10 });
```

This will select from the `MyModel` table with a limit of 10 and an offset of 5.

> **Note**
> The `limit` property will tell the database to only retrieve that number of rows (in MSSQL, this would be `SELECT TOP N` or `FETCH NEXT N ROWS`). The `offset` property will skip N rows before retrieving the results. For MSSQL 2008 (and earlier) users, Sequelize will offer offset support by nesting queries to simulate offset behavior for compatibility and completeness.

Now that we have finished referencing Sequelize's methodologies for querying and manipulating data, we can now go over the more advanced options when defining a model. These options can change the way Sequelize will transform data internally, filter queried data, and adjust naming conventions, allowing you to better adapt Sequelize's behavior to your company/project's requirements.

Advanced Sequelize options for defining models

When defining a model, within Sequelize, the last input parameter for the `init()` and `define()` methods offers us a way to fine-tune our project's requirements and Sequelize's behavior. These parameter options are useful for situations such as when we need to construct Sequelize in a pre-existing environment that does not adhere to Sequelize's naming conventions (for example, a column named `PersonIsMIA` as opposed to Sequelize's `"PersonIsMia"` convention).

sequelize

A copy (or new) instance of Sequelize to associate with the model. Sequelize will return an error if this field is not provided (except when using the `sequelize.define` method). Useful for querying across data centers or even databases.

modelName

Explicitly defines the model's name with a string. This would be the first parameter in Sequelize's `define()` method. If you are using ES6 class definitions, the default for this value would be the class name.

defaultScope/scopes

An object for values that will set the model's default scope and set applicable scopes for the model, respectively. Scopes can be useful for code organization or enforcing a basic access control list as a default behavior. We will go into detail about scoping in a later chapter.

omitNull

Setting this Boolean value to `true` will tell Sequelize to omit any columns that have a `null` value when saving a record.

timestamps

This option allows us to control Sequelize's behavior for adding `createdAt` and `updatedAt` timestamp columns for the model. The default value for this setting is `true` (Sequelize will create timestamp columns).

> **Note**
>
> You can always override the default settings for the `createdAt` and `updatedAt` attributes by defining them explicitly within your model. Sequelize will know to use those attributes for timestamp-related columns.

paranoid

This Boolean option, when set to `true`, will prevent Sequelize from deleting the data (by default) and adds a `deletedAt` timestamp column. The `timestamps` option must be set to `true` in order to make `paranoid` applicable. The default value for `paranoid` is `false`.

The following query will perform a "soft deletion":

```
await Post.destroy({
  where: {
    id: 1
  }
});
```

This query will update the `Post` record of ID 1 and update the `deletedAt` column. If we wanted to remove the record from the database (instead of updating it), we would use the `force` parameter, as illustrated in the following code snippet:

```
await Post.destroy({
  where: {
```

```
    id: 1
  },
  force: true
});
```

This would perform a `delete` query versus an `update` query on the database.

createdAt/updatedAt/deletedAt

This option will rename the `createdAt`, `updatedAt`, and `deletedAt` attributes, respectively. If you provide camel-cased values and the underscored option is set to `true`, Sequelize will automatically convert the column's casing. Setting the value as `false` instead of a string will tell Sequelize to disable its default behavior for that respective column.

underscored

By default, Sequelize will create columns using camel case (for example, `updatedAt`, `firstName`, and so on). If you prefer underscores or snake case (for example, `updated_at`, `first_name`, and so on), then you would set this value to `true`.

freezeTableName

As previously mentioned, Sequelize will pluralize table names derived from the model's name by default. Setting this value to `true` would prevent Sequelize from transforming the table's name.

tableName

Explicitly defines the table name for Sequelize to use when creating SQL queries. A typical use case for this option is when you are integrating Sequelize into a pre-existing database/schema or when the pluralization is incorrectly set.

name

An object with two available options to define singular and plural names to use when associating this model with others. A clearer explanation, and an example, will be provided when we go over model associations and relations in a later chapter, but you can see an overview of the two options here:

- `singular`—The name to use when referencing a single instance from a model (defaults to `Sequelize.Utils.singularize(modelName)`)
- `pluralize`—The name to use when referencing multiple instances of a model (defaults to `Sequelize.Utils.pluralize(modelName)`)

schema

Defines the model's schema (this would be referenced as `search_path` in Postgres). Not all databases support schemas, and some will refer to schemas as databases entirely.

engine

Applicable to MySQL only, this is where you can define your table's engine type (typically `InnoDB` or `MyISAM`). The default is `InnoDB`.

charset

Specifies the table's charset. Useful for when your table's contents can be deterministically defined to a set of characters that could help reduce database size (if you do not need universal encodings and only Latin characters, then you would use a Latin-derived charset).

collation

Specifies the table's collation (sorting and ordering rules for the characters).

comment

Adds a comment to the table (if applicable to the DBMS).

initialAutoIncrement

Sets the initial `AUTO_INCREMENT` value for applicable dialects (MySQL and MariaDB).

hooks

An object with keys mapped to hooks (or life cycle events). The values may be a function or an array of functions. We will go into details about hooks in a later chapter.

validate

An object to define model validations. We will go into detail about validations in the next chapter.

indexes

An array of objects that define table indices' definitions. These indices are created when calling `sync()` or using the migration tool. Each object has the following options:

- name—The name of the index (Sequelize will default to the model's name and applicable fields joined by an underscore).

- type—A string value for defining the index's type (only for MySQL/MariaDB). Typically, this is where you would define FULLTEXT or SPATIAL indices (UNIQUE as well, but there is a dialect-agnostic option for creating unique indices).

- unique—Setting this value to true would create a unique index.

- using—The USING clause value for the index's SQL statement. A few examples would be BTREE (typically, a DBMS will use this index type as the default), HASH (MySQL/MariaDB/Postgres only), and GIST/GIN (Postgres only).

- operator—Defines an operator to use for this index (primarily used for Postgres but can be used in other dialects).

- concurrently—Setting this to true offers a way of creating indices without writing locks (Postgres only).

- fields—An array of index fields to define for the model. Refer to the *Index fields* section, next.

Index fields

Each index definition's fields value can be one of the following:

- A string indicating the name of the index

- Sequelize literal object functions (for example, sequelize.fn())

- An object with the following keys:

  - attribute—A string value for the column to index

  - length—Defines the length for a prefix index (if applicable to your DBMS)

  - order—Determines whether the sorting should be ascending or descending

  - collate—Defines the collation for the column

A quick example is provided here to illustrate how to use some of these advanced options when defining a Sequelize model:

```
class User extends Model { }

User.init({
    name: DataTypes.STRING,
}, {
    sequelize,
    modelName: 'User',
    omitNull: true,
```

```
        // renames deletedAt to removedAt
        deletedAt: 'removedAt',

        // start with ID 1000
        initialAutoIncrement: 1000,

        validate: {
            isNotBob() {
                if (this.name === 'bob') {
                    throw new Error("Bob is not allowed to be a
                                    user.");
                }
            }
        },
        indexes: [
            { unique: true, fields: ['name'] }
        ],
    });
```

Summary

In this chapter, we went through a detailed overview of the various parameters and configuration settings for defining models with Sequelize. We also learned how to use the Sequelize CLI to automatically generate models' definition (and data) files and how to migrate those definitions to a database. This chapter has also covered the various attribute types provided by Sequelize, as well as the methodologies for querying or updating data from Sequelize to the database.

In the next chapter, we will go over model validations, establishing foreign relationships, and how to constrain your data to meet your project's requirements.

Part 2 –
Validating, Customizing, and
Associating Your Data

In this part, you will take a deeper look into Sequelize's model attributes and add validations, custom column types, and related associated models. You will explore hooks, JSON, and Blob types, along with transactions.

This part comprises the following chapters:

- *Chapter 3, Validating Models*
- *Chapter 4, Associating Models*
- *Chapter 5, Adding Hooks and Lifecycle Events to Your Models*
- *Chapter 6, Implementing Transactions with Sequelize*
- *Chapter 7, Handling Customized, JSON, and Blob Data Types*

3
Validating Models

It is important to maintain consistency and integrity within databases. Databases often use some form of constraint stipulation to ensure consistency. Typically, these constraints consist of checking for a range of values, such as minimum string length, uniqueness, or existence. Integrity for databases involves managing the associations and relations between symbiotic records. This involves cascading updates and deletions of referenced records (for example, setting the associated identity columns to NULL when the referenced record has been deleted). Consistency and integrity are not mutually exclusive to one another, but the two patterns help to ensure organization.

> **Note**
> The term consistency refers to ensuring that only valid data will be written and read from the database (especially within the context of accessing data concurrently). Integrity refers to data that conforms to a set of rules, constraints, or triggers before it is inserted or read.

While most database engines handle both consistency and integrity, there are some limitations as far as consistency is concerned. If you wanted to perform validations against a third-party source outside of the database's scope, you would need to either build (or install) an extension for the database that adds support or use a central code base to help manage these validations.

Sequelize offers built-in validation for various data types to help with the ergonomics of a project. Some validations require manual configuration, such as checking to see whether a text value matches an email pattern, or manual input for certain validations, such as numerical (or date) ranges.

Validations can be performed using two methodologies within Sequelize:

- We can execute validations across the entire record involving multiple attributes
- We can invoke validations for each specific attribute

We will explore how Sequelize performs validations in this chapter to maintain consistency and integrity within databases. This chapter will cover the following topics:

- Using validations as constraints
- Creating custom validation methods
- Executing validations while performing asynchronous operations
- Handling validation errors

> **Note**
>
> Sequelize will internally use a validation library called `validator.js`. This chapter will go over the validations that Sequelize extends explicitly. For a complete list of validations that can be used, you may refer to the `validator.js` repository at `https://github.com/validatorjs/validator.js`.

Technical requirements

You can find the code files for this chapter at: `https://github.com/PacktPublishing/Supercharging-Node.js-Applications-with-Sequelize/tree/main/ch3`

Using validations as constraints

There are certain validations that Sequelize will use as both a validation and a constraint. These parameters are configurable in the attribute's options as a sibling to the `validate` parameters. Constraints are defined and guarded by the database, whereas a validation will be handled by Sequelize and the Node.js runtime exclusively. Here is a list of constraints made available from Sequelize.

allowNull

The `allowNull` option will determine whether to apply NOT NULL to the definitions of columns for the database. The default value is `true`, which will allow columns to have a value of `null`. There are a couple of caveats to keep in mind when using validations with the `allowNull` constraint:

- If the `allowNull` parameter is set to `false` and the attribute's value is `null`, then the custom validations will not run. Instead, a **ValidationError** will be returned without making a request to the database.
- If the `allowNull` parameter is set to `true` and the attribute's value is `null`, then the built-in validators will not be invoked, but the custom validators will still execute.

The following is an illustration of the various validation states that will cause Sequelize to behave accordingly, depending on the `allowNull` parameter:

```
User.init({
  age: {
    type: Sequelize.INTEGER,
    allowNull: true,
    // if the age value is null then this will be ignored
    validate: {
      min: 1
    }
  },
  name: {
    type: DataTypes.STRING,
    allowNull: true,
    validate: {
      // even if the name's value is null, the
        customValidator will still be invoked
      customValidator(value) {
        if (value === null && (this.age === null ||
            this.age < 18)) {
          throw new Error("A name is required unless the
                          user is under 18 years old");
        }
      }
    }
  },
  email: {
    type: DataTypes.STRING,
    allowNull: false,
    validate: {
      // if the email value is null then this will not be
        invoked
      customValidator(value) {
        // ...
      }
    }
  }
}, { sequelize });
```

In the previous example, in the first column, `age`, Sequelize will perform a validation check to make sure the numerical value is not less than one. The next column, `name`, will invoke a custom validation function that checks whether the attribute's new value is `null` and checks for the user's age if so. The last column, `email`, demonstrates that Sequelize will not invoke validations if the `allowNull` flag is set to `false` and the value itself is `null`.

You can customize NOT NULL errors by adjusting the `notNull` parameter in the validate config of the attribute as follows:

```
User.init({
  email: {
    type: DataTypes.STRING,
    allowNull: false,
    validate: {
      notNull: {
        msg: 'Please enter your e-mail address'
      }
    }
  }
}, { sequelize });
```

Otherwise, Sequelize will return the error message that was sent from the database.

unique

Setting this parameter to `true` will have Sequelize build a unique constraint on the applicable column within the database if you are using Sequelize's `sync` option. If there was a unique constraint violation, Sequelize will return an error type of `SequelizeUniqueConstraintError`. Here's a quick example of how to use `unique` (you may allow nullable values for uniqueness as well):

```
MyModel.init({
  email: {
    type: DataTypes.STRING,
    // by default allowNull is true
    allowNull: false,
    unique: true
  }
}, { sequelize });
```

As a general rule of thumb, you should use constraints over validations, wherever applicable, since this option will be applied to the database as well. In cases where a constraint is not applicable, we can use one of Sequelize's built-in validations.

> **Note**
>
> When setting `allowNull` to `true` on a `unique` attribute, the database will allow multiple records with the same NULL value on that attribute. This is intentional from the DBMS's side and can be mitigated by explicitly adding constraints to a `unique` index such as the following:
>
> CREATE UNIQUE INDEX idx_tbl_uniq ON tbl (a, (b IS NULL)) WHERE b IS NULL

Built-in validations

These validations are performed within the Node.js runtime and not from the database. Sequelize will extend the functionality of `validator.js` with its own set of validators.

is (regex), not (notRegex), and equals

The `is` and `not` validation parameters can either be a literal regular expression or an array, with the first entry as a string literal for the regular expression and the second entry for regular expression flags. The `equals` parameter is a string value that performs a strict comparison check for exact matching.

The following is an example of how to use all three for a model:

```
MyModel.init({
  foo: {
    type: DataTypes.STRING,
    validate: {
      is: /^[a-z]+$/i
      // can also be written as:
      // is: ['^[a-z]+$', 'i']
    }
  },
  bar: {
    type: DataTypes.STRING,
    validate: {
      not: /^[a-z]+$/i
      // can also be written as:
      // not: ['^[a-z]+$', 'i']
    }
```

```
  },
  foobar: {
    type: DataTypes.STRING,
    validate: {
      // ensure 'foobar' is always equaled to 'static
         value'
      equals: 'static value'
    }
  }
}, { sequelize });
```

isEmail

This validation will ensure that the attribute's value matches the rules according to RFC 2822, which can be reviewed at `https://datatracker.ietf.org/doc/html/rfc2822`.

isUrl

This will validate whether the attribute's value is an actual URL with various protocols, hostnames (IP and FQDN), and a maximum length.

isIP, isIPv4, or isIPv6

This validates whether the attribute's value matches how an IP value should look. The `isIP` validation accepts both v4 and v6 formats.

isAlphanumeric, isNumeric, isInt, isFloat, and isDecimal

All inputs for validations are sent to the `validator.js` library as a literal string. These validators will ensure the input can parse into the respective validation.

max or min

These apply to numerical attributes only. They add a maximum or minimum numerical value respectively for the attribute's validations.

isLowercase or isUppercase

These check to see whether every letter in the attribute's value uses the proper case.

isNull, notNull, or notEmpty

This validates whether the value is `null` or not. The `notEmpty` validator will validate whether there are any spaces, tabs, or newlines within the value.

contains, notContains, isIn, or notIn

These contain-related validators will perform a substring check on the value. The in-related validators accept any value within an array parameter. For example, see the following:

```
MyModel.init({
  foo: {
    type: DataTypes.STRING,
    validate: {
      isIn: [['red', 'yellow', 'green']]
    }
  },
  bar: {
    type: DataTypes.STRING,
    validate: {
      contains: 'foo'
    }
  }
}, { sequelize });
```

len

The `len` validator accepts an array with two parameters for its input. The parameters are for checking the value's length against a minimum and maximum number respectively. To create a validation for a value's length with a minimum length of 1 and a maximum length of 40, it would look as follows:

```
MyModel.init({
  foo: {
    type: DataTypes.STRING,
    validate: {
      len: [1, 40]
    }
  }
}, { sequelize });
```

isUUID

This validator can check whether a value is in accordance with being a unique identifier. You can specify the version (3, 4, or 5) as the input parameter or a literal string value of `all` to accept any UUID version.

isDate, isAfter, or isBefore

The `isDate` validator will determine whether a value is *date-like*. The `isAfter` and `isBefore` validators will perform a temporal comparison against the date that you are trying to validate against. The default input for comparison is `new Date()`. The following is a quick example:

```
MyModel.init({
  expiration: {
    type: DataTypes.DATE,
    validate: {
      isAfter: '2060-01-01'
      // for "now"
      // isAfter: true
    }
  }
}, { sequelize });
```

> **Note**
> The input for `isBefore` and `isAfter` is a string that conforms to any applicable date that can be parsed by JavaScript. For examples in compatible formats, you may refer to this link: `https://developer.mozilla.org/en-US/docs/Web/JavaScript/Reference/Global_Objects/Date/parse`.

Now that we have gone through several examples of how validations are applied to a Sequelize model's attributes, we can update several files within the Avalon Airlines project.

Applying validations to our project

In the following example, we will add validations for our Airplane model's `planeModel` and `totalSeats` attributes. We can begin by opening the `models/airplane.js` file and adding the following validations:

- For the `planeModel` attribute, add a `notEmpty` validation since all plane models require a value that is not `null` nor an empty string.

- On the `totalSeats` attribute, add a minimum validation of `1` as the argument's value since every plane must have at least one seat available for customers.

The updated file should look something similar to this:

```
const { Model } = require('@sequelize/core');

module.exports = (sequelize, DataTypes) => {
  class Airplane extends Model {
    static associate(models) {
    }
  };

  Airplane.init({
    planeModel: {
      type: DataTypes.STRING,
      validate: {
        notEmpty: {
          msg: 'Plane types should not be empty'
        }
      }
    },
    totalSeats: {
      type: DataTypes.INTEGER,
      validate: {
        min: {
          args: 1,
          msg: 'A plane must have at least one seat'
        }
      }
    }
  }, {
    sequelize,
    modelName: 'Airplane',
  });

  return Airplane;
};
```

Next, we will want to modify the `models/boardingticket.js` file, and add a `notEmpty` validator as follows:

```
const { Model } = require('@sequelize/core');
module.exports = (sequelize, DataTypes) => {
  class BoardingTicket extends Model {
    static associate(models) {
    }
  };

  BoardingTicket.init({
    seat: {
      type: DataTypes.STRING,
      validate: {
        notEmpty: {
          msg: 'Please enter in a valid seating arrangement'
        }
      }
    }
  }, {
    sequelize,
    modelName: 'BoardingTicket',
  });

  return BoardingTicket;
};
```

The last file to edit within this section will be the `models/customer.js` file. The name attribute will require a `notEmpty` validator and the email attribute will need an `isEmail` validator as follows:

```
const { Model } = require('@sequelize/core');

module.exports = (sequelize, DataTypes) => {
  class Customer extends Model {
    static associate(models) {
    }
  };
```

```
Customer.init({
  name: {
    type: DataTypes.STRING,
    validate: {
      notEmpty: true,
      msg: 'A name is required for the customer'
    }
  },
  email: {
    type: DataTypes.STRING,
    validate: {
      isEmail: true,
      msg: 'Invalid email format for the customer'
    }
  }
}, {
  sequelize,
  modelName: 'Customer',
});

  return Customer;
};
```

After going through the list of built-in validations, we can now learn how to build our own validations, and how to use custom validations across the entire model.

Creating custom validation methods

Sequelize gives us the ability to create our own validations simply by adding a function to the `validate` parameter on attributes or within the `validate` parameter on the model's options (the second input parameter for the `Model.init()` function).

If we wanted to create our own validation to restrict our users from using `password` as a password, we would write a solution similar to this:

```
MyModel.init({
  password: {
    type: DataTypes.STRING,
    validate: {
```

```
      notLiteralPassword(value) {
        if (value === 'password') {
          throw new Error("Your password cannot be
                            'password'");
        }
      }
    }
  }
}, { sequelize });
```

Even though you can check the value on other attributes within a custom attribute validator, it is considered good practice to declare a model custom validator, which we will demonstrate shortly, when involving more than one attribute for validation, which we will demonstrate shortly.

We have one more model file to add validations for. The `models/flightschedule.js` file will need to validate that the origin airport is not the same as the destination airport. First, we will need to import Sequelize and add a list of available airports:

```
const { Model } = require('@sequelize/core');
const availableAirports = [
  'MIA',
  'JFK',
  'LAX'
];
```

Next, add in the module exports and model class extension lines:

```
module.exports = (sequelize, DataTypes) => {
  class FlightSchedule extends Model {
    static associate(models) {
    }
  };
```

Creating custom attribute validators

Then, we can initialize our model with attribute definitions that have validations associated with them. We will want to add the `isIn` validator to the `originAirport` and `destinationAirport` attributes:

```
FlightSchedule.init({
```

```
    originAirport: {
      type: DataTypes.STRING,
// examples of custom attribute validators
      validate: {
        isIn: {
          args: [availableAirports],
          msg: 'Invalid origin airport'
        }
      }
    },
    destinationAirport: {
      type: DataTypes.STRING,
      validate: {
        isIn: {
          args: [availableAirports],
          msg: 'Invalid destination airport'
        }
      }
    },
    departureTime: {
      type: DataTypes.DATE,
      validate: {
        isDate: {
          args: true,
          msg: 'Invalid departure time'
        }
      }
    }
  }, {
    sequelize,
    modelName: 'FlightSchedule',
    validate: {
```

Adding a custom model validator

Now, we can add our custom model validator here. We will create a function that will check the values against the `originAirport` and `destinationAirport` attributes. If both of the values are identical, then we will mark the destination as invalid and throw an error:

```
validDestination() {
    const hasAirportValues = this.originAirport !==
    null && this.destinationAirport !== null;
    const invalidDestination = this.originAirport ===
    this.destinationAirport;;

    if (hasAirportValues && invalidDestination) {
      throw new Error("The destination airport cannot
                      be the same as the origin");
    }

  }
```

For the last step, we will close any objects or functions, and return the class back to the export:

```
    }
  });

  return FlightSchedule;
};
```

You may have noticed that we pass through the `validDestination` validator if both values are `null`. The `isIn` validator will still execute and return an error due to there not being a valid value.

Executing validations while performing asynchronous operations

Sometimes, your validations will require you to fetch an associated model's record, call a third-party application, or some other form of request that waits for a response.

Suppose we were in a situation where we have to ensure that there was a completed and active payment before creating or updating a customer's membership points. As long as any payment was still considered in good standing, that customer should be able to update their membership. We would use the `async` and `await` keywords to help us execute these requests and wait for the responses for validation:

```
Membership.init({
  points: {
    type: DataTypes.INTEGER,
  }
}, {
  sequelize,
  validate: {
    async accountIsActive() {
      const payments = await Payments.find({
        where: { status: 'complete', expired: false }
      });

      if (payments.length < 1) {
        throw new Error("Invalid membership");
      }
    }
  }
});
```

> **Note**
>
> The `async` and `await` keywords work on custom attribute validators as well.

It is important to note that if you run Sequelize queries within a life cycle event, then those queries will execute under a different transaction than the parent model. For instance, if we started a transaction and inside its scope, we created the payment entry and then tried to create the membership entry, the `await Payments.find(...)` line would not be able to see the recently created record. To remedy this issue, we can pass a Sequelize transaction to the `transaction` parameter when calling `create`. The following is a very generic but high-level example:

```
const tx = await sequelize.transaction();

try {
  await Payment.create({ status: 'complete', expired: false });

  await Membership.create({
```

```
    points: 100,
    // without the following line the `await
       Payments.find()` call in
    // ...accountIsActive will not find the previously
       created entry
    transaction: tx
  });

  await t.commit();
} catch (err) {
  await t.rollback();
}
```

Handling validation errors

Using `FlightSchedule` from the *Creating custom validation methods* section, we will go over how to handle validation errors when invoking the `validate`, `update`, and `create` methods. Let's presume that we called a `createFlightSchedule` method that looks as follows:

```
const { ValidationError } = require('@sequelize/core');
// other imports and code...

async function createFlightSchedule() {
  try {
    await FlightSchedule.create({
      originAirport: 'JAX',
      destinationAirport: 'JFK',
      departureTime: '2030-01-01T00:00:00.000+00:00'
    });
  } catch (err) {
    if (err instanceof ValidationError) {
      console.log(err.errors);
    } else {
      console.log(err);
    }
  }
}
```

```
}

    return FlightSchedule;
};
```

By default, the returned error from `ValidationError` should be similar to this (you may see additional fields listed):

```
[
  ValidationErrorItem {
    message: 'Invalid origin airport',
    type: 'Validation error',
    path: 'originAirport',
    value: 'JAX',
    origin: 'FUNCTION',
    instance: FlightSchedule {
      dataValues: [Object],
      _previousDataValues: [Object],
      uniqno: 1,
      _changed: [Set],
      _options: [Object],
      isNewRecord: true
    },
    validatorKey: 'isIn',
    validatorName: 'isIn',
    validatorArgs: [ [Array] ],
    original: Error: Invalid origin airport {
      validatorName: 'isIn',
      validatorArgs: [Array]
    }
  }
]
          origin airport'}
]
```

Alternatively, we could manually check for validation before attempting to create or modify the record using the instance's `validate()` method as follows:

```
async function createFlightSchedule() {
  try {
    const schedule = FlightSchedule.build({
      originAirport: 'JAX',
      destinationAirport: 'JFK',
      departureTime: '2030-01-01T00:00:00.000+00:00'
    });

    await schedule.validate();
  } catch (err) {
    console.log(err);
  }
}
```

The result would return an error object similar to this:

```
{
  errors: [
    ValidationErrorItem {
      message: 'Invalid origin airport',
      type: 'Validation error',
      path: 'originAirport',
      value: 'JAX',
      origin: 'FUNCTION',
      instance: [FlightSchedule],
      validatorKey: 'isIn',
      validatorName: 'isIn',
      validatorArgs: [Array],
      original: [Error]
    }
  ]
}
                          the same as the origin']

}
```

So, now that our data is *consistent*, what about *integrity*? In the next chapter, we will go over what Sequelize has to offer us for creating (and manipulating) associations and the various ways of relating models.

Summary

In this chapter, we added validations to our models using some of Sequelize's built-in validators and adding our own custom validation methods. We then moved on to handling and performing asynchronous methods inside of custom validations. Once we were able to invoke validations properly, we were then able to practice handling errors for validations.

In the next chapter, we will be covering another part of adding consistency and integrity to our database, which is handling relations and associations for our models. Validations will ensure integrity on a database row level and associations can be used to ensure integrity across tables and other rows.

4
Associating Models

Other than using validations to ensure consistency within our database, we can also create associations between two tables to ensure symbiotic relationships are maintained and updated. Databases maintain these relationships by creating **foreign key references** that hold metadata as to which table and column the foreign key is associated with. This metadata is what maintains integrity for the database. If we were to update a foreign key's value without a proper reference, we would have to perform a separate query to update all of the rows that contained a reference to the foreign key to its new value.

For instance, we have three tables: `customers`, `products`, and `receipts`. The `receipts` table would have two columns (in addition to others) with each referencing a column on the `customers` and `products` table, respectively. If we wanted to update a product's identification column, we would have to just modify the applicable product's identification value. Then, the rows referencing the product within `receipts` would update automatically. Without a foreign reference, we would have to explicitly update the `receipts` table after updating the product's identification.

> **Note**
> Traditionally, foreign keys would reference a primary key column or some form of identification column, but you are not limited to just those columns.

Relations between models can be managed by Sequelize automatically, or in a configurable way, for adopting pre-existing databases. Mapping relations between models can help ORMs form efficient queries depending on the environment by **eager loading** or **lazy loading**.

This chapter will cover the following topics:

- Association methods
- Relationship patterns
- Querying associations with eager loading and lazy loading
- Using advanced association options
- Applying associations to Avalon Airlines

Technical requirements

You can find the code files for this chapter at https://github.com/PacktPublishing/ Supercharging-Node.js-Applications-with-Sequelize/tree/main/ch4

Association methods

There are a few options for creating relational mappings with ORMs. Defining the relations through an ORM can help build your database with the proper attributes and columns automatically, manage associated validations (for example, checking to see whether there is strictly only one related record), and perform optimization patterns on queries when fetching or inserting data. Sequelize offers support for four association patterns:

- **HasOne** – A one-to-one association where the *foreign key references the child* model. The attribute is defined on the parent model.

- **BelongsTo** – A one-to-one association where the *foreign key references the parent* model. The attribute is defined on the child model.

- **HasMany** – A one-to-many association where the *foreign key references the parent* model. The attribute is defined on the child model.

- **BelongsToMany** – A many-to-many association where a separate model (called a *junction table*) will store the references of the associated models.

Sequelize will follow a pattern for creating methods on models with associations. Depending on the relationship, there can be get, set, add, create, remove, and count as the prefix for the method's name following with the association's name (singular or pluralized wherever applicable).

In this section, we will go over the list of associations with their corresponding methods. Once we have gone through the association overview, then we can begin with the patterns for the relationships overview. Throughout this section, we will be using the concept of actors and plays/movies/jobs to help us grasp the fundamentals of associative properties and behavior on models. These examples are for illustrative purposes only and should not be included within our project's code base.

> **Note**
> You can add a where clause statement (along with other finder parameters) within the get association methods, such as the following:
>
> ```
> Actor.getJobs({
>     where: { category: 'Action' },
>     limit: 10, offset: 20, /* etc. */
> });
> ```

hasOne

The `hasOne` association will generate `get`, `set`, and `create` methods for the associating model. Suppose we had the following association and instance:

```
Actor.hasOne(Job);
const actor = await Actor.create({ ... });
```

We can use the `createJob` method to insert and set the job with the actor:

```
await actor.createJob({ name: '...' });
```

The `setJob` method will update the association of the actor and the job from a `Job` instance:

```
const job = await Job.create({ name: '...' });
await actor.setJob(job);
```

You may use the `set` prefix method to remove an association as well with a `null` value:

```
await actor.setJob(null);
```

belongsTo

Let's change our previous example's model to this:

```
Actor.belongsTo(Job);
```

The `belongsTo` association will generate the exact same methods on the same model as the `hasOne` association. For further explanation, this association will not create `setActor` on the `Job` model but will create the `setJob` method on the `Actor` model still.

hasMany

The `hasMany` association will generate the following prefixed methods: `get`, `set`, `create`, `count`, `has`, `add`, and `remove`. The `get` and `set` methods are similar to the previous example except that the suffix of the method's name will be a pluralized version of the model's name:

```
Actor.hasMany(Job);

let jobs = await Job.findAll();

await Actor.setJobs(jobs);
await Actor.getJobs();
```

The `create` prefix method will still only create one record at a time and therefore the model's name is still singular-cased:

```
await Actor.createJob({ name: '…' });
```

We can also check to see whether a relationship already exists with the `has` method:

```
const job = await Job.findOne();
// true or false boolean value
const hasJob = await Actor.hasJob(job);
// using jobs from our previous example
const hasAllJobs = await Actor.hasJobs(jobs);
```

We can add one or multiple associations using the `add` method like so:

```
await Actor.addJob(job);
await Actor.addJobs(jobs);
```

To retrieve how many associations we have for a model, we can invoke the `count` method:

```
// will return 2 following the examples in this section
await Actor.countJobs();
```

Removing the associations can be done with the `remove` methods:

```
await Actor.removeJob(job);
await Actor.removeJobs(jobs);
```

belongsToMany

Next, we change the association to `belongsToMany`:

```
Actor.belongsToMany(Job, { through: '...' });
```

The `belongsToMany` association will generate the same methods on the same model as the previous `hasMany` example, similar to how `belongsTo` generated the same methods as the `hasOne` association.

Renaming associations

You can modify how Sequelize will generate the method names by creating an alias to the association using the `as` parameter:

```
Actor.hasOne(Job, {
  as: 'gig'
```

```
});
const actor = await Actor.create({ … });
const gig = await Job.create({ … });
actor.createGig({ … });
actor.setGig(gig);
actor.hasGig(gig);
```

> **Note**
>
> You can manually set the identifier of a relationship directly to the attribute and Sequelize will update the value with the `save` method. However, if you have made any changes within the associated records, their information will not be updated by calling the associating instance's `save` method. Changes to the actual associations would need to be done from their own instance.

Now that we know how to apply association methods to our models, we can go over the various relationship patterns to help us get a better understanding of where, and when, these associations are coupled. In the next section, we will go into detail on the relationship patterns that Sequelize supports along with examples for each pattern.

Relationship patterns

In this section, we will go over the details of each type of relation (except Super-Many-To-Many, which is discussed in a later section), and how to use Sequelize to define the associations. After that, we will update the Avalon Airlines project's models with associations.

We can combine several association patterns to define a relationship pattern. Sequelize supports four relationship patterns:

- **One-to-One** – We would use the *hasOne* and *belongsTo* associations together.

- **One-to-Many** – The *hasMany* and *belongsTo* associations are used for this pattern.

- **Many-to-Many** – Two *belongsToMany* associations are used for this pattern.

- **Super-Many-to-Many** – Two *One-to-Many* relations where the *One* models are still considered symbiotic. This relationship will be explained in further detail in the *Creating Super Many-to-Many relationships* section.

One-to-One

The One-to-One relational pattern involves the `hasOne` and `belongsTo` associations for the models. The difference between the two associations is which table will have the identification column.

As an example, we have an `Airplane` and `BoardingTicket` model. Since the `Airplane` model would no longer be involved with `BoardingTicket`, after the flight has been completed, we can omit the memorization of the boarding ticket from the `Airplane` model's table. This means that `Airplane` would not need a `hasOne` association, but `BoardingTicket` will still need a `belongsTo` association.

To define a One-to-One relationship, we would define our models like so:

```
const A = sequelize.define('A', { … });
const B = sequelize.define('B', { … });
A.hasOne(B);
B.belongsTo(A);
```

Using Sequelize's `sync` command would yield the following queries:

```
CREATE TABLE IF NOT EXISTS "b" (
  /* … */
);
CREATE TABLE IF NOT EXISTS "b" (
  /* … */
  "aId" INTEGER REFERENCES "a" ("id") ON DELETE SET NULL ON
UPDATE CASCADE
  /* … */
);
```

> **Note**
>
> Without calling `A.hasOne(B)`, Sequelize would not know how to eager load from model A to B (but would be able to eager load from model B to A).

There are several options that you can pass as a second parameter for tuning the behavior of the associations:

- `onUpdate` – Tells the DBMS how to handle updated foreign relationships. Possible values are `CASCADE`, `RESTRICT`, `NO ACTION`, `SET DEFAULT`, and `SET NULL`. The default value for this option is `CASCADE`.
- `onDelete` – Same as `onUpdate` but for handling deleted foreign relationships. The default for this option is `SET NULL`.
- `foreignKey` – Accepts a literal string value or an object with the same options as an attribute when defining models (`name`, `allowNull`, `unique`, etc.).

- `sourceKey` – The name of the column, from the source table, to use as identification for the foreign key column's value. By default, Sequelize will use the source table's attribute that has a `primaryKey: true` parameter. If your model contains no explicit `primaryKey` attribute, then Sequelize will use the default `id` attribute. Applicable to `hasOne` and `hasMany` associations.

- `targetKey` – Similar to `sourceKey` except this value will reference the column from the target table as opposed to the source table. Applicable to `belongsTo` associations.

Here are a few examples of how to use these options:

```
A.hasOne(B, {
    onUpdate: 'SET NULL',
    onDelete: 'CASCADE',
    foreignKey: 'otherId'
});
B.belongsTo(A);

A.hasOne(B, {
    onUpdate: 'CASCADE',
    onDelete: 'SET NULL',
    foreignKey: { name: 'otherId' }
});
B.belongsTo(A);
```

You can use the second options interchangeably between models A and B:

```
A.hasOne(B);
B.belongsTo(A, {
    onUpdate: 'SET NULL',
    onDelete: 'CASCADE',
    foreignKey: 'otherId'
});

A.hasOne(B);
B.belongsTo(A, {
    onUpdate: 'CASCADE',
    onDelete: 'SET NULL',
    foreignKey: { name: 'otherId' }
});
```

By default, Sequelize will make One-to-One relations optional, but if we wanted to require a relationship between the two models, then we would define `allowNull` as `false` in the association options like so:

```
A.hasOne(B, {
  foreignKey: { allowNull: false }
});
```

One-to-Many

This relational pattern will only create a foreign reference column on the `belongsTo` model. Defining an attribute with the `hasMany` association helps Sequelize with data retrieval optimization and adding helper functions to the parent model. The options in the second parameter are the same as a One-to-One relationship.

Suppose we had `Employees` that belonged to `Organization`. With Sequelize, the code would be similar to the following:

```
Organization.hasMany(Employee);
Employee.belongsTo(Organization);
```

This would execute these couple of queries:

```
CREATE TABLE IF NOT EXISTS "Organizations" (
  /* ... */
);
CREATE TABLE IF NOT EXISTS "Employees" (
  /* ... */
  "OrganizationId" INTEGER REFERENCES "Organizations" ("id") ON
DELETE SET NULL ON UPDATE CASCADE,
  /* ... */
);
```

Many-to-Many

This relationship will use an associative entity to keep references between two models. Some other names for an associative entity are junction table, junction model, cross-reference table, and pairing table. With `sequelize.sync()`, Sequelize will automatically create a junction model for you, but we still have the option of defining our own junction table for situations where we want to add more attributes, constraints, life cycle events, and so on.

In this example, we have employees that have tasks assigned to them. Employees can work on multiple tasks and tasks can require many employees:

```
Employee.belongsToMany(Task, { through: 'EmployeeTasks' });
Task.belongsToMany(Employee, { through: 'EmployeeTasks' });
```

This will execute the following query:

```
CREATE TABLE IF NOT EXISTS "EmployeeTasks" (
    "createdAt" TIMESTAMP WITH TIME ZONE NOT NULL,
    "updatedAt" TIMESTAMP WITH TIME ZONE NOT NULL,
    "EmployeeId" INTEGER REFERENCES "Employees" ("id") ON
DELETE CASCADE ON UPDATE CASCADE,
    "TaskId" INTEGER REFERENCES "Tasks" ("id") ON DELETE
CASCADE ON UPDATE CASCADE,
    PRIMARY KEY ("EmployeeId","TaskId")
);
```

> **Note**
>
> Many-to-Many relationships will use CASCADE as the default behavior for managing foreign keys and relationships on both updates and deletions.

If we wanted to be more explicit in our definitions or wanted to add a custom attribute to the junction model, we can define the junction model and relations like so:

```
// Employee and Task are pre-defined for brevity
const EmployeeTasks = sequelize.define('EmployeeTasks', {
    EmployeeId: {
        type: DataTypes.INTEGER,
        references: {
            model: Employee,
            key: 'id'
        }
    },
    TaskId: {
        type: DataTypes.INTEGER,
        references: {
            model: 'Tasks', // string literal values work here
                            too
```

```
        key: 'id'
      }
    },
    SomeOtherColumn: {
        type: DataTypes.STRING
    }
});


Employee.belongsToMany(Task, {
    through: EmployeeTasks
});


Task.belongsToMany(Employee, {
    through: EmployeeTasks
});
```

Other than the `through` parameter, Many-to-Many offers a parameter called `uniqueKey`, which will allow you to name a reference column. By default, Sequelize will create the junction table with a unique key composed of both referencing columns (`employeeId` and `taskId`). If you wish to change this behavior, you may set the `unique` attribute parameter to `false` in the junction model's definition.

Using custom foreign key definitions

When, and how, to use `sourceKey` and `targetKey` properly can be confusing at first. The `hasOne` and `hasMany` associations will reference themselves from the Parent model (target model) to the Child model (source model); another way of saying this is, "This child is mine through name, marriage, and so on." The `belongsTo` association will reference the Parent model, or "I belong to this parent through name, marriage, and so on."

We reference these models as *source* and *target* models since parent and child could be misleading and would imply some form of hierarchy. Associations do not require a hierarchy; they just form relationships.

Note

Attributes that are defined as references are required to have a unique constraint applied to them. This can be done by adding `unique: true` to the attribute's options and using Sequelize's `sync()` method.

For an example of how to configure the source and target keys, we will first define our models:

```
const Actor = sequelize.define('Actors', {
    name: {
        type: DataTypes.TEXT,
        unique: true
    }
});


const Role = sequelize.define('Roles', {
    title: {
        type: DataTypes.TEXT,
        unique: true
    }
});


const Costume = sequelize.define('Costumes', {
    wardrobe: {
        type: DataTypes.TEXT,
        unique: true
    }
});
```

Using these roles, we will go through examples of using `hasOne`, `hasMany`, `belongsTo`, and `belongsToMany` separately.

Using hasOne

The following code will create an attribute called `actorName` on the `Roles` model, and the value for that attribute will be associated with the actor's name (instead of the actor's ID attribute):

```
Actor.hasOne(Role, {
    sourceKey: 'name',
    foreignKey: 'actorName'
});
```

Using hasMany

We would use the same options for the `hasMany` association. The following code will create an attribute called `roleTitle` on the `Costumes` model, which will be associated with the role's title:

```
Roles.hasMany(Costumes, {
    sourceKey: 'title',
    foreignKey: 'roleTitle'
});
```

Using belongsTo

The `belongsTo` association works a bit differently. Instead of referencing from the source model, `belongsTo` will reference from the target model like so (this would yield the same results as the previous `Actors.hasOne(Roles, ...)` code):

```
Roles.belongsTo(Actors, {
    targetKey: 'name',
    foreignKey: 'actorName'
});
```

In other words, the foreign keys will be placed on the model that is creating the association when using `belongsTo`, and for the `hasOne`/`hasMany` associations, the foreign keys are placed on the other model that is not invoking the association method.

Using belongsToMany

The `belongsToMany` association accepts both the target and the source keys as parameters to configure the references. On the movie set, an actor could have multiple costumes for all of their different scenes. We can illustrate this relationship in Sequelize like so:

```
Costumes.belongsToMany(Actors, {
    through: 'actor_costumes',
    sourceKey: 'name',
    targetKey: 'wardrobe'
});
```

This will create a junction table called `actor_costumes` with two reference columns being `actorsName` and `costumesWardrobe`, referencing the Actor and Costume model, respectively.

Now that we have gone over definitions, options, use cases, and examples for Sequelize's association patterns, and the main three relational patterns, we can start practicing including those relations for when we select or modify records.

Querying associations with eager loading and lazy loading

Sequelize offers two different methods of querying associations depending on how you wish to query the data: eager loading and lazy loading. With eager loading, you would load all of the associated data at once. The lazy loading method will load the associations per query as they are called upon from the code. It is easier to explain eager loading than lazy loading but to see the benefits of eager loading, we will need to go over lazy loading first.

> **Note**
>
> You may have heard of the "N+1 select problem" with other ORM frameworks; this is referring to the lazy loading method (although, not mutually exclusive) and how selecting an association per row could be hazardous to your application's performance.

Lazy loading

Sequelize tries to make no presumptions about your intent and will initially select only the model's data. We will need to explicitly call the associations if we want to transverse through the model's related data. A good use case for lazy loading would be querying related data conditionally (for example, we may not want to fetch movie reviews until after the movie is released). Lazy loading would look similar to this:

```
const actor = await Actor.findOne();
// SELECT * FROM jobs WHERE actorId=?
const job = await Actor.getJob();

let reviews = [];
if (job.isDone) {
  // SELECT * FROM reviews WHERE jobId=?
  reviews = await job.getReviews({
    where: { published: true }
  });
}
```

Eager loading

Usually, you would use this form of loading when you have a lot of associations or a lot of rows returned from the main table. Referencing the previous example, let's say we replaced getJob with getJobs and called getReviews per job, like so:

```
const jobs = await Actor.getJobs();
let reviews = [];
```

```
jobs.map(async job => {
  if (job.isDone) {
    let jobReviews = await job.getReviews({
      where: { published: true }
    });
    reviews = reviews.concat(jobReviews);
  }
});
```

If the actor ever became too famous and had hundreds of jobs, we could see how quickly the number of queries could become too cumbersome for the system. One way to prevent this is by using the eager loading method, which will include the associated data at the top-level query using JOIN statements. Let us convert the previous example into an eager-loaded query with Sequelize by beginning to define our completed jobs association:

```
const completedJobs = {
    model: Job,
    as: 'CompletedJobs',
    where: {
        completed: true
    },
    include: {
        model: Review,
        where: {
            published: true
        }
    }
}
```

This first include parameter will load the Job model, set an alias to CompletedJobs, add a where clause for the completed flag, and then call a nested association from Job to Review (along with a published where clause for the review).

Next, we need to define our incomplete jobs association:

```
const incompleteJobs = {
    model: Job,
    as: 'IncompleteJobs',
    where: {
```

```
            completed: false
        }
    }
}
```

The second parameter is a simpler alias association for `Job` with an inverted `where` clause from `CompletedJobs`.

The idea here is to query the completed and incomplete jobs separately since we only want to include reviews from jobs that are done. Now, we can query our actor with the jobs and reviews:

```
const actor = await Actor.findOne({
    include: [ completedJobs, incompleteJobs ]
});
```

This will generate an SQL query similar to this (some selected columns have been omitted for brevity):

```
SELECT
    `Actor`.*,

    `CompletedJobs`.`title` AS `CompletedJobs.title`,
    `CompletedJobs`.`completed` AS `CompletedJobs.completed`,
    `CompletedJobs->Reviews`.`id` AS `CompletedJobs.Reviews.
     id`,
    `CompletedJobs->Reviews`.`published` AS `CompletedJobs.
     Reviews.published`,

    `IncompleteJobs`.`title` AS `IncompleteJobs.title`,
    `IncompleteJobs`.`completed` AS `IncompleteJobs.completed`

FROM (
    SELECT `Actor`.`id`, `Actor`.`name`, `Actor`.`createdAt`,
    `Actor`.`updatedAt`
    FROM `Actors` AS `Actor`
    LIMIT 1
) AS `Actor`

LEFT OUTER JOIN `Jobs` AS `CompletedJobs` ON
    `Actor`.`id` = `CompletedJobs`.`ActorId` AND
    `CompletedJobs`.`completed` = true
```

```
LEFT OUTER JOIN `Reviews` AS `CompletedJobs->Reviews` ON
    `CompletedJobs`.`id` = `CompletedJobs->Reviews`.`JobId` AND
    `CompletedJobs->Reviews`.`published` = true

LEFT OUTER JOIN `Jobs` AS `IncompleteJobs` ON
    `Actor`.`id` = `IncompleteJobs`.`ActorId` AND
    `IncompleteJobs`.`completed` = false;
```

Then, concatenate the completed and incomplete jobs:

```
const jobs = [].concat(
  actor.CompletedJobs,
  actor.IncompleteJobs
);
```

Now we can iterate through jobs and display the reviews if applicable:

```
jobs.forEach(job => {
  const reviews = job.Reviews || [];
  // display reviews here
});
```

Now that we have the fundamentals of the two load types for Sequelize, we can now start venturing into more advanced concepts when associating data. In the next section, we will go over more advanced query patterns for associations: Super Many-to-Many associations and polymorphic associations.

Using advanced association options

Sequelize offers a variety of tricks to help communicate with your database's relations properly. Some of these methods will help query associations in a more organized and ergonomic way. Other methods will offer us a way to compose the database's schematics for more advanced relationship patterns. In this section, we will be going over examples of how to manage complex many-to-many relationships using the Super Many-to-Many pattern, define scoped associations, and query polymorphic associations.

Using scopes with associations

Scopes are a way to define a namespace with a default set of parameters, or parameters that override previously applied scopes to a query. Associations may have defined scopes to help with organization of the code base. A key difference between scopes for associations and models is that the association scope's parameters are applicable for the WHERE clause. Model scopes can define the WHERE, LIMIT, and OFFSET clauses, for example.

The following is an example of querying associations with scopes:

```
const Worker = sequelize.define('worker', { name: DataTypes.
STRING });
const Task = sequelize.define('task', {
  title: DataTypes.STRING,
  completed: DataTypes.BOOLEAN
});


Worker.hasMany(Task, {
    scope: {
        completed: true
    },
    as: 'completedTasks'
});


const worker = await Worker.create({ name: "Bob" });
await worker.getCompletedTasks();
```

Sequelize will add a mixin for the `worker` instance called `getCompletedTasks()`, which would invoke a query similar to this:

```
SELECT `id`, `completed`, `workerId`
FROM `tasks` AS `task`
WHERE `task`.`completed` = true AND `task`.`workerId` = 1;
```

The `task`.`completed` = true part was automatically added from Sequelize from the scope's definition. An alternative way of defining the same scope is shown here:

```
Task.addScope('completed', {
    where: { completed: true }
});


Worker.hasMany(Task.scope('completed'), {
  as: 'completedTasks'
});
```

When creating scoped associations, Sequelize will automatically add default values for those parameters when calling the `create` or `add` mixins. As an example, we know a worker has already completed a task and wanted to insert the association like so:

```
const worker = Worker.findOne();
await worker.createCompletedTask({ title: 'Repair Cluster' });
```

Sequelize will execute a similar query when creating a completed task via `worker`:

```
INSERT INTO "tasks" (
    "id", "title", "completed"
) VALUES (
    DEFAULT, 'Repair Cluster', true, 1
) RETURNING *;
```

The `completed` attribute has been automatically set to `true` for when we want to add a completed task. The same behavior would be exhibited if we were to use the `add` mixin.

Using the scope parameter on a `belongsToMany` association would apply the scope to the target model instead of the junction mode. If you wish to apply a scope on the junction model instead, you would add the scope parameter inside of the `through` configuration like so:

```
const WorkerTask = sequelize.define('WorkerTask', {
  published: DataTypes.BOOLEAN
});

Worker.belongsToMany(Task.scope('completed'), {
  through: {
    model: WorkerTasks,
    scope: { published: true }
  },
  as: 'CompletedAndPublishedTask'
});
```

Creating Super Many-to-Many relationships

Suppose we owned a store and wanted to maintain lists of associations between employees and customers through transactions. Typically, we can define this sort of relationship by adding a `belongsToMany` association on the `Employee` and `Customer` model using the `Transaction` model as the junction table.

Let us start with the definitions of these models to use throughout this section:

```
const Employee = sequelize.define('employee', {
  name: DataTypes.STRING,
});

const Customer = sequelize.define('customer', {
  name: DataTypes.STRING
});

const Transaction = sequelize.define('transaction', {
  id: {
    type: DataTypes.INTEGER,
    primaryKey: true,
    autoIncrement: true,
    allowNull: false
  },
  couponCode: DataTypes.STRING
});
```

You may have noticed that the `Transaction` model has the `id` attribute explicitly defined as the primary key. This will prevent Sequelize from using the composition keys of `employeeId` and `customerId` as the primary key, which is required for establishing Super Many-to-Many relationships.

There are two ways to create a Many-to-Many relationship with these three models. The common way would be to use the `belongsToMany` association like so:

```
Employee.belongsToMany(Customer, { through: Transaction });
Customer.belongsToMany(Employee, { through: Transaction });
```

The other method is to use `hasMany` and `belongsTo` on both of the associating models:

```
Employee.hasMany(Transaction);
Transaction.belongsTo(Employee);

Customer.hasMany(Transaction);
Transaction.belongsTo(Customer);
```

These two methods will yield the same schematic result for the junction table (creating `employeeId` and `customerId` on the junction model). However, when you try to eager load the data, you may run into several issues depending on how you are trying to query the data.

With the `belongsToMany` associations, we may query our models in the following way (however, this will not work for the `hasMany` and `belongsTo` method):

```
Employee.findAll({ include: Customer });
Customer.findAll({ include: Employee });
```

Including the junction model from the associated models would not work for the `belongsToMany` approach, but the following code would work for the `hasMany` and `belongsTo` method:

```
Employee.findAll({ include: Transaction });
Customer.findAll({ include: Transaction });
```

Trying to include associated models through the junction model will only work with the `hasMany` and `belongsTo` method. The following code will not work for the `belongsToMany` pattern:

```
Transaction.findAll({ include: Employee });
Transaction.findAll({ include: Customer });
```

In order to be able to use all of the various forms of eager loading for these models, we can implement the Super Many-to-Many pattern by combining the two associated methods such as the following:

```
Employee.belongsToMany(Customer, { through: Transaction });
Customer.belongsToMany(Employee, { through: Transaction });
Employee.hasMany(Transaction);
Transaction.belongsTo(Employee);
Customer.hasMany(Transaction);
Transaction.belongsTo(Customer);
```

Declaring our associations like this would allow us to query associative data via the junction model, or the associated models themselves, without constraint or stipulations. Deeply nested includes are also supported natively with the Super Many-to-Many relationship.

Using polymorphic associations

When we have two or more associative models targeting the same foreign key on a junction table we can use a polymorphic association pattern for that scenario. You may think of polymorphic associations as some type of generic interfacing for associated data.

Suppose we owned an online retail store and wanted to store reviews for both widgets and gizmos under one review table. Initially, we would want to use `hasMany` and `belongsTo` associations, but this would cause Sequelize to generate two columns on the junction model (`widgetId` and `gizmoId`) instead of one for a generic pattern. Semantically, this would not make sense either since a review is not associated with a widget *and* a gizmo product.

First, we will need to define our `Widget` and `Gizmo` models:

```
const Widget = sequelize.define('Widget', {
  sku: DataTypes.STRING,
  url: DataTypes.STRING
});


const Gizmo = sequelize.define('Gizmo', {
  name: DataTypes.STRING
});
```

Next, we will define our `Review` model like so:

```
const Review = sequelize.define('Review', {
  message: DataTypes.STRING,
  entityId: DataTypes.INTEGER,
  entityType: DataTypes.STRING
}, {
    instanceMethods: {
        getEntity(options) {
if (!this.entityType) return Promise.resolve(null);

const mixinMethodName = `get${this.entityType}`;
            return this[mixinMethodName](options);
        }
    }
});
```

The `instanceMethods` parameter will create a `getEntity` function per instance, which will check to see whether `entityType` is null. If there is an entity type, then we can call the associated mixin function by adding a `get` prefix to the entity type's value.

Now we can establish our relationships as shown here:

```
Widget.hasMany(Review, {
  foreignKey: 'entityId',
  constraints: false,
  scope: {
    entityType: 'Widget'
```

```
    }
});


Review.belongsTo(Widget, { foreignKey: 'entityId',
                           constraints: false });


Gizmo.hasMany(Review, {
  foreignKey: 'entityId',
  constraints: false,
  scope: {
    entityType: 'Gizmo'
  }
});
Review.belongsTo(Gizmo, { foreignKey: 'entityId',
                          constraints: false });
```

For each association, we will use `entityId` as `foreignKey`, and since the junction model references more than one table, we cannot set a reference constraint on that table (which is why we set `constraints` to `false`):

```
Review.addHook("afterFind", findResult => {
if (!Array.isArray(findResult)) findResult = [findResult];
  for (const instance of findResult) {
    if (instance.entityType === "Widget" && instance.Widget
        !== undefined) {
      instance.entity = instance.Widget;
    } else if (instance.entityType === "Gizmo" && in
              stance.Gizmo !== undefined) {
      instance.entity = instance.Gizmo;
    }
  }
});
```

To query the associations, do the following:

```
const widget = await Widget.create({ sku: "WID-1" });
const review = await widget.createReview({ message: "it works!"
});
```

```
// the following should be true
console.log(review.entityId === widget.id);
```

Polymorphism allows us to retrieve the widget or gizmo without being pre-deterministic in our queries by calling our instance method, getEntity:

```
const entity = await review.getEntity();

// widget and entity should be the same object and return
   "true" for deep comparison checking
const isDeepEqual = require('deep-equal');
console.log(isDeepEqual(widget, entity));
```

In order to load our data eagerly, we would include the associated models like any other eager-loaded query:

```
const reviews = await Review.findAll({
    include: [Widget, Gizmo]
});
for (const review of reviews) {
    console.log('Found a review with the following entity:
                ', review.entity.toJSON());
}
```

The afterFind hook will automatically associate the create instance to the entity key for each review.

Since we are referencing more than one table to one target column, we will need to be extra careful when querying the junction model. For instance, if both Widget and Gizmo had an ID of 5 and a review had entityType of Gizmo, and we queried reviews with Review.findAll({ include: Widget }), then the Widget instance would be eager loaded into Review regardless of entityType.

Sequelize will not automatically infer the entity's type from the model's name. Luckily, our afterFind life cycle event will assign the entity value properly. It is recommended to always use the abstracted methods (for example, getEntity) over Sequelize's mixins (for example, getWidget, getGizmo, etc.) in order to avoid ambiguity.

So far, we have shown an example of a One-to-Many relationship, but what about a Many-to-Many? Using the previous example models, we can add an associated model called Categories, which would look like the following:

```
const Category = sequelize.define('Category', {
    name: DataTypes.STRING
```

```
    }, {
        instanceMethods: {
            getEntities(options) {
                const widgets = await this.getWidgets(options);
                const gizmos = await this.getGizmos(options);
                return [].concat(widgets, gizmos);
            }
        }
    });
```

Now, we can create our junction model for a Many-to-Many relationship by assigning two foreign key columns:

```
const CategoryEntity = sequelize.define('CategoryEntity', {
    categoryId: {
        type: DataTypes.INTEGER,
        unique: 'ce_unique_constraint'
    },
    entityId: {
        type: DataTypes.INTEGER,
        unique: 'ce_unique_constraint',
        references: null
    },
    entityType: {
        type: DataTypes.STRING,
        unique: 'ce_unique_constraint'
    }
});
```

The ce_unique_constraint lines will tell Sequelize that all three of these attributes belong to the same composited unique key. The null reference for entityId will ensure that Sequelize will not create a reference constraint for that column.

Next, we can define our relations for Widget and Gizmo along with a helper method. We will assign a common parameter configuration along with a function for amending a scope to the parameter:

```
const throughJunction = {
    through: {
        model: CategoryEntity,
```

```
        unique: false
    },
    foreignKey: 'entityId',
    constraints: false
};

function scopeJunction(scope) {
    let opts = throughJunction;

    opts.through.scope = {
        entityType: scope
    };

    return opts;
}
```

Then, we can assign our relationships to the applicable models:

```
Widget.belongsToMany(Category, scopeJunction('Widget'));
Category.belongsToMany(Widget, throughJunction);

Gizmo.belongsToMany(Category, scopeJunction('Gizmo'));
Category.belongsToMany(Gizmo, throughJunction);
```

Calling a method such as `widget.getCategories()` would execute a similar query to this:

```
SELECT
    `Category`.`id`,
    `Category`.`name`,
    `CategoryEntity`.`categoryId` AS `CategoryEntity.
     categoryId`,
    `CategoryEntity`.`entityId` AS `CategoryEntity.entityId`,
    `CategoryEntity`.`entityType` AS `CategoryEntity.
     entityType`,
FROM `Categories` AS `Category`
INNER JOIN `CategoryEntities` AS `CategoryEntity` ON
    `Category`.`id` = `CategoryEntity`.`categoryId` AND
    `CategoryEntity`.`entityId` = 1 AND
    `CategoryEntity`.`entityType` = 'Widget';
```

Now that we have learned how to operate with associations and relationships for Sequelize, we can begin making some modifications to our Avalon Airlines project.

Applying associations to Avalon Airlines

Luckily, the models for the project are simple and won't require the amount of effort as defining a Super Many-to-Many relationship. Within these next several model updates, this book will demonstrate what to modify only for the `class` model block (the rest of the contents within each file should remain the same).

Starting in alphabetical order, we will begin modifying the `models/airplane.js` file's `class` block by adding a relationship to `FlightSchedule`:

```
class Airplane extends Model {
  static associate(models) {
this.FlightSchedules =
this.hasMany(models.FlightSchedule);
  }
};
```

Next, we can edit the `models/boardingticket.js` file's `class` block and add a `Customer` and `FlightSchedule` relationship:

```
class BoardingTicket extends Model {
  static associate(models) {
    this.Customer = this.belongsTo(models['Customer']);
    this.FlightSchedule = this.
belongsTo(models['FlightSchedule']);
  }
};
```

Customers will now have many boarding tickets; the `models/customer.js` file's `class` block should now look like this:

```
class Customer extends Model {
  static associate(models) {
this.BoardingTickets =
this.hasMany(models.BoardingTicket);
  }
};
```

Flight schedules will belong to a specific airplane, and they will have many boarding tickets. We can edit the `models/flightschedule.js` file's `class` block to match the following example:

```
class FlightSchedule extends Model {
  static associate(models) {
    this.Airplane = this.belongsTo(models['Airplane']);
    this.BoardingTickets = this.
hasMany(models['BoardingTicket']);
  }
};
```

Since we are not executing `sync({ force: true })` when initializing Sequelize, we will need to generate a migrations file and add the necessary references for their respective models. We can use the Sequelize CLI tool to generate a new migrations file using the `migration:generate` subcommand:

```
sequelize migration:generate --name add-references
```

Sequelize will notify you on the new file that it has generated a migration file with a message similar to this:

```
New migration was created at /Users/book/
migrations/20211031155604-add-references.js .
```

The prefixed number on the filename will be different from what appears on your screen, but if we look into the `migrations` directory, then we will see a newly generated file. We can quickly overwrite the file's contents.

At the top of the file, we will want to include `DataTypes` and start our migration's up block:

```
const { DataTypes } = require("@sequelize/core");

module.exports = {
  up: async (queryInterface, Sequelize) => {
```

We can now add the `FlightSchedule` model's reference for the `Airplane` model by adding a column first and then adding the constraint:

```
    await queryInterface.addColumn('FlightSchedules',
'AirplaneId', {
      type: DataTypes.INTEGER,
    });
```

```
await queryInterface.addConstraint('FlightSchedules', {
  type: 'foreign key',
  fields: ['AirplaneId'],
  references: {
    table: 'Airplanes',
    field: 'id'
  },
  name: 'fkey_flight_schedules_airplane',
  onDelete: 'set null',
  onUpdate: 'cascade'
});
```

Next, we will want to do the same for `BoardingTicket` and its related models, `Customer` and `FlightSchedule`:

```
  await queryInterface.addColumn('BoardingTickets',
'CustomerId', {
    type: DataTypes.INTEGER,
  }

);    await queryInterface.addConstraint('BoardingTickets', {
    type: 'foreign key',
    fields: ['CustomerId'],
    references: {
      table: 'Customers',
      field: 'id'
    }
  ,   name: 'fkey_boarding_tickets_customer',
    onDelete: 'set null',
    onUpdate: 'cascade'
  });

  await queryInterface.addColumn('BoardingTickets',
                              'FlightScheduleId', {
    type: DataTypes.INTEGER,
  });

  await queryInterface.addConstraint('BoardingTickets', {
    type: 'foreign key',
```

```
    fields: ['FlightScheduleId'],
    references: {
      table: 'FlightSchedules',
      field: 'id'
    },
    name: 'fkey_boarding_tickets_flight_schedule',
    onDelete: 'set null',
    onUpdate: 'cascade'
  });
```

Now, we can close the up block and start our down block for migration reversal support:

```
  },

  down: async (queryInterface, Sequelize) => {
```

We will need to remove the constraints first, then the columns, and finally, close the down block and exported object like so:

```
    await queryInterface.removeConstraint(
      'FlightSchedules', 'fkey_flight_schedules_airplane'
    );

    await queryInterface.removeConstraint(
      'BoardingTickets', 'fkey_boarding_tickets_customer'
    );

    await queryInterface.removeConstraint(
      'BoardingTickets',
      'fkey_boarding_tickets_flight_schedule'
    );

    await queryInterface.removeColumn('FlightSchedules',
      'AirplaneId');
    await queryInterface.removeColumn('BoardingTickets',
      'CustomerId');
    await queryInterface.removeColumn('BoardingTickets',
    'FlightScheduleId');
```

```
    }
};
```

In our console, we can migrate these new changes with the following command:

```
sequelize db:migrate
```

Sequelize will confirm that the migration has been completed, and our models are officially related to each other through associations. Throughout this book, we will use the lessons learned from this chapter for including associated data within our queries, but for now, we will move on to the next lesson.

Summary

In this chapter, we went over defining relations of models using associative properties along with some advanced options and relational patterns, and we went over the differences between eager loading and lazy loading. At the end of this chapter, we took our lessons from the previous chapter, *Validating Models*, and added validations, associations, and migrations for our Avalon Airlines project.

> **Note**
> If you ever get stuck on associations and need a quick reference, the related material can be found here: https://sequelize.org/docs/v6/core-concepts/assocs/.

In the next chapter, we will go over Sequelize's hook feature (also known as a life cycle event), how to define hooks for models, and what would be some good use cases for life cycle events.

5

Adding Hooks and Lifecycle Events to Your Models

ORM typically provides a way for us to be able to transform states, or objects, throughout events that occur when executing certain operations. These methods are often referred to as hooks, lifecycle events, object lifecycles, or even callbacks (the latter is *not* often used within the Node.js community due to a nomenclature conflict against Node.js' native environment). Usually, these methods have a temporal prefix (for example, `before` and `after`) preceding an event's name.

There are no strict rules as to what an ORM requires as an event throughout its entire lifecycle. The events typically included within an ORM are called: validation, save, create, update, and destroy. Other ORM frameworks offer a wider scope of events or more granular control, such as before/after connecting to your database, defining your models, and calling a finder query.

Sequelize categorizes hooks into global and local hooks. Global hooks are for defining default lifecycle events for every model, enforce events (referred to as permanent hooks in Sequelize), and connection-related events. The local hooks entail lifecycle events defined on models for instances/records.

In this chapter, we will go over the following:

- The order of operations for lifecycle events
- Defining, removing, and executing lifecycle events
- Using lifecycle events with associations and transactions

> **Note**
>
> You can always reference Sequelize's code base to maintain an up-to-date list of available lifecycle events here: `https://sequelize.org/docs/v6/other-topics/hooks/`.

Technical requirements

You can find the code files for this chapter at `https://github.com/PacktPublishing/Supercharging-Node.js-Application-with-Sequelize/blob/main/ch5`.

Order of operations for lifecycle events

Lifecycle events are an important feature when we want to introduce project-specific behaviors/constraints that extend beyond a database engine's scope. Knowing the lifecycle events is only half of the equation, and the other half consists of knowing when those lifecycle events are triggered.

Suppose we were given the task to offer all of our products for free to employees. The first action could be adding a `beforeValidate` hook that would set the transaction's subtotal to 0 if the user was an employee. That's easy for us, but unfortunately a nightmare for the accounting department. A better approach would be to add an additional item that represents the employee discount, using the `beforeValidate` or `beforeCreate` hook.

The real answer in knowing which lifecycle events to use depends on the project's requirements. From our previous example, some transactions require moving legal tender, which involves charging the employee and then providing a refund/credit as a separate transaction. In this case, we would not be able to use `beforeValidate` nor `beforeCreate`, but `afterCreate` could be applicable. Under the context of Sequelize, knowing where to place your code's logic is knowing the order of operations for lifecycle events.

In Sequelize, lifecycle events follow the `before/after` preface style for hook names, like other ORM frameworks. All of Sequelize's *connection* lifecycle events are defined on the `sequelize` object itself, and all of the *instance* event types are defined on models. The *model* event types can be defined in both areas. The exception to these rules is when we want to define an instance event for all of the models globally (examples will be provided in the following section). Here is a table listing lifecycle events in the order that they are executed along with a signature for the callback function:

Hook definitions sorted by lifecycle execution

Event name	Event type	Requires sync*
`beforeConnect(config)` `beforeDisconnect(connection)`	Connection	No
`beforeSync(options)` `afterSync(options)`	Connection	No
`beforeBulkSync(options)` `afterBulkSync(options)`	Connection	No
`beforeQuery(options, query)`	Connection	No

Event name	Event type	Requires sync*

`beforeDefine(attributes, options)`
 	
`afterDefine(factory)`
	Connection (Model)	Yes

`beforeInit(config, options)`
 	
`afterInit(sequelize)`
	Connection (Model)	Yes

`beforeAssociate({ source, target, type }, options)`
 	
`afterAssociate({ source, target, type, association }, options)`
	Connection (Model)	Yes

`beforeBulkCreate(instances, options)`
 	
`beforeBulkDestroy(options)`
 	
`beforeBulkRestore(options)`
 	
`beforeBulkUpdate(options)`
	Model	No

`beforeValidate(instance, options)`	Instance	No

`afterValidate(instance, options)`
 	
`validationFailed(instance, options, error)`
	Instance	No

`beforeCreate(instance, options)`
 	
`beforeDestroy(instance, options)`
 	
`beforeRestore(instance, options)`
 	
`beforeUpdate(instance, options)`
 	
`beforeSave(instance, options)`
 	
`beforeUpsert(values, options)`
	Instance	No

`afterCreate(instance, options)`
 	
`afterDestroy(instance, options)`
 	
`afterRestore(instance, options)`
 	
`afterUpdate(instance, options)`
 	
`afterSave(instance, options)`
 	
`afterUpsert(created, options)`
	Instance	No

Event name	Event type	Requires sync*
afterBulkCreate(instances, options) afterBulkDestroy(options) afterBulkRestore(options) afterBulkUpdate(options)	Instance	No
afterQuery(options, query)	Connection	No
beforeDisconnect(connection) afterDisconnect(connection)	Connection	No

*These lifecycle events will be triggered only if `sequelize.sync()` is invoked.

The majority of these lifecycle events are explicative in corresponding with their Sequelize function (for example, `beforeSave` for `Model.save()`). However, there are two types of events that are implicative and may not be clear initially. The first one is the `restore` events related to paranoid models (where records are considered `delete` with a column flag as opposed to being physically deleted). The second one is the `Upsert` events that are invoked for `create`, `update`, and `save`-related methods, indicating to us whether a record was newly created or updated from a pre-existing record.

Where Sequelize differentiates from other ORM lifecycle events is, in addition to *instance* and *connection*-related events, Sequelize will also provide hooks surrounding *finder* methods (for example, `findAll` and `findOne`). The following is a list with a brief explanation of each finder event:

- `beforeFind(options)`: Occurs before any transformation that occurs to options from Sequelize internally

- `beforeFindAfterExpandIncludeAll(options)`: An event that is triggered after Sequelize expands the *include* attributes (for example, setting proper defaults for specific associations)

- `beforeFindAfterOptions(options)`: Before the finder method invokes the query and after Sequelize is finished hydrating/transforming options

- `afterFind(instances, options)`: Returns a single instance or an array of instances after a finder method is finished querying

- `beforeCount(options)`: This event will trigger before the `count()` instance method queries the database

Now that we have a better understanding of which hooks are available to use and the order of execution through the lifecycle, we can begin building our models with lifecycle events attached to them.

Defining, removing, and executing lifecycle events

There are several ways to attach lifecycle events to models and Sequelize's behavior. Each of these methods allows us to change the attribute values that are derived from the hook's arguments as pass-by-reference. For example, you can add additional properties to the instances returned in `afterFind` by simply updating the attributes on the objects from within the lifecycle method. By default, Sequelize will treat lifecycle events as synchronous operations, but if you need asynchronous capabilities, you can return a `Promise` object or an `async` function.

Defining instance and model lifecycle events

Instance and model lifecycle events can be defined in several ways, including defining these events as a local hook (defined directly from the model itself). There are several ways to define a local hook; we will start with the basic example of declaring hooks during the initialization of a model:

```
class Receipt extends Model {}
Receipt.init({
  subtotal: DataTypes.DECIMAL(7, 2)
}, {
  hooks: {
    beforeValidate: (receipt, options) => {
      if (isEmployee(receipt.customer)) {
        receipt.subtotal = 0;
      }
    }
  }
});
// or with the define() method
sequelize.define('Receipts', {
  subtotal: DataTypes.DECIMAL(7, 2)
}, {
  hooks: {
    beforeValidate(receipt, options) => { … })
  }
});
```

To define the same exact hook outside of initialization, we can either use the addHook() method or invoke the corresponding lifecycle method directly. This method provides an easy way for plugins and adapters to integrate with your models after defining them. The following is a simple example of how to use this method:

```
function employeeDiscount(receipt, options) {
  if (isEmployee(receipt.customer)) {
    receipt.subtotal = 0;
  }
}
class Receipt extends Model {}
Receipt.init({ subtotal: DataTypes.DECIMAL(7, 2) });
Receipt.addHook('beforeValidate',employeeDiscount);
// or you can use the direct method:
Receipt.beforeValidate(employeeDiscount);
```

The previous examples provided illustrations for synchronous events. An example of asynchronous hooks involves returning a Promise (as previously stated), like so:

```
async function employeeDiscount(receipt, options) {
  if (!customerIsEmployee) {
    return;
  }

  const discountTotal = await
  getDiscountFromExternalAccountingService(employeeId);
    receipt.subtotal = discountTotal;
}
Receipt.addHook('beforeValidate', employeeDiscount);
// or...
Receipt.beforeValidate(employeeDiscount);
```

To throw an error from a synchronous lifecycle event, you can return a rejected Promise object:

```
Receipt.beforeValidate((receipts, options) => {
  return Promise.reject(new Error("Invalid receipt"));
});
```

For organizational purposes, you can declare names for your lifecycle events using the `addHook()` or direct methods:

```
Receipt.addHook('beforeValidate', 'checkForNegativeSubtotal',
(receipt, options) => { … });
// or
Receipt.beforeValidate('checkForNegativeSubtotal', (receipt,
options) => {…});
```

These examples provide us with methods for assigning lifecycle events on the local scope of the model itself. If we wanted to define lifecycle events on a global scope (applicable to all models), we would use the Sequelize constructor to do so:

```
const sequelize = new Sequelize(…, {
  define: {
    hooks: {
      beforeValidate() {
      // perform some kind of data transformation/validation
      }
    }
  }
});
```

This will generate a default `beforeValidate` hook for models that do not define their own `beforeValidate` hooks. If you wish to run a global hook, regardless of whether the model has its own definition, we can define **permanent hooks**:

```
sequelize.addHook('beforeValidate', () => { … });
```

Even if a model has its own `beforeValidate` hook definition, Sequelize will still execute the global hook. If we have a global and local hook associated with the same lifecycle event, then Sequelize will execute the local hook(s) first followed by the global hook(s).

For model-specific event types (such as `bulkDestroy` and `bulkUpdate`), Sequelize will not execute individual delete and update hooks per row by default. To modify this behavior, we can add a `{ individualHooks: true }` option for when we call these methods, like so:

```
await Receipt.destroy({
  where: { … },
  individualHooks: true
});
```

> **Note**
> Using the `{ indvidualHooks: true }` option could cause a decrease in performance, depending on whether Sequelize will need to retrieve rows, store the rows/additional information in memory (for example, `bulkDestroy` and `bulkUpdate` but not `bulkCreate`), and execute individual hooks per record.

Removing lifecycle events

Some projects will require conditionally invoking lifecycle events. For instance, we may have some sort of validation to check whether a user is still eligible for replying to a comment on a forum. This validation is appropriate for a production environment but not necessary for a development environment.

One method would be to create a conditional logic surrounding the hook definition – for example, the following:

```
if (!isDev) {
  User.addHook('beforeValidate', 'checkForPermissions', …);
}
```

This would technically work, but what if we had several stipulations, such as sending an order email in the `afterCreate` hook or refunding an order in production only? We would have a lot of "`if` statements" throughout the code base. Sequelize offers a method to remove lifecycle events to help organize this type of workflow called `removeHook`.

We could load all of the lifecycle events as we normally would, but if our environment is at the development stage, then we can run through all of our models and remove the applicable hooks. All of these granular tunings can be organized in one function given the `removeHook` method:

```
function removeProductionOnlyHooks() {
  // this will remove all matching hooks by event type and
     name
  User.removeHook('beforeValidate', 'checkForPermissions');

  // this will remove all beforeValidate hooks on the User
     model
  User.removeHook('beforeValidate');

  // this will remove all of the User model's hooks
  User.removeHook();
}
```

```
 // load our models...
if (isDev) {
  removeProductionHooksOnly();
}
```

Removing lifecycle events is useful for timed behavior in an application or for removing explicit debugging hooks. The next section will help us understand the order of operation when executing lifecycle events and when a specific lifecycle event will be executed.

Executing lifecycle events

Sequelize will run the corresponding/applicable lifecycle events based on the method that you are invoking. Using our previous `Transactions` model example, if we were to run `Transactions.create({ ... })`, then Sequelize would automatically run the following lifecycle events (in sequential order):

1. `beforeValidate`
2. `afterValidate/validationFailed`
3. `beforeCreate`
4. `beforeSave`
5. `afterSave`
6. `afterCreate`

One caveat to keep in mind for executing lifecycle events is that when you are using the `update()` method, it is important to keep in mind that Sequelize will not execute the lifecycle events unless an attribute's value has changed.

For instance, this will not call the corresponding lifecycle events:

```
var post = await Post.findOne();
await Post.update(post.dataValues, {
  where: { id: post.id }
});
```

Since the values did not change, Sequelize will ignore the lifecycle events. If we wanted to enforce this behavior, we could add a `hooks: true` parameter to the update's configuration:

```
await Post.update(post.dataValues, {
  where: { id: post.id },
  hooks: true
});
```

Now that we have the basics of how to define, remove, and execute lifetime events, we can move on to the nuances of utilizing hooks with associations and transactions.

Using lifecycle events with associations and transactions

As the default behavior, Sequelize will execute lifecycle events without associating a transaction with any database queries that are invoked within the lifecycle's scope. However, sometimes our project requires transactions to be used within lifecycle events, such as an accountant's ledger or creating log entries. Sequelize offers a transaction parameter when calling certain methods, such as update, create, destroy, and findAll, that will allow us to use a transaction that was defined outside of the lifecycle's scope to be used within the lifecycle itself.

> **Note**
> When calling beforeDestroy and afterDestroy on a model, Sequelize will intentionally skip destroying any associations with that model unless the onDelete parameter is set to CASCADE and the hooks parameter is set to true. This is due to Sequelize needing to explicitly delete each association row by row, which could cause congestion if we are not careful.

If we were to write a naive accounting system and wanted to create logging entries as a separate ledger, we would first define our models like so:

```
class Account extends Model {}
Account.init({
    name: {
        type: DataTypes.STRING,
        primaryKey: true,
    },
    balance: DataTypes.DECIMAL,
});

class Book extends Model {}
Book.init({
    from: DataTypes.STRING,
    to: DataTypes.STRING,
    amount: DataTypes.DECIMAL,
});
```

Then, we can add our `Ledger` model, which is a copy of the `Book` model with a naive reference column (for brevity) and a signature column, to indicate that the transaction was approved by an external source:

```
class Ledger extends Model {}
Ledger.init({
    bookId: DataTypes.INTEGER,
    signature: DataTypes.STRING,
    amount: DataTypes.DECIMAL,
    from: DataTypes.STRING,
    to: DataTypes.STRING,
});
```

To automate the `Ledger` workflow, we can add an `afterCreate` hook to our Book model to record the account balance changes:

```
Book.addHook('afterCreate', async (book, options) => {
    const from = await Account.findOne(book.from);
    const to = await Account.findOne(book.to);

    // pretend that we have an external service that "signs"
        our transactions
    const signature = await getSignatureFromOracle(book);

    await Ledger.create({
        transactionId: book.id,
        signature: signature,
        amount: book.amount,
        from: from.name,
        to: to.name,
    });
});
```

Now, when we create a new booking entry, we can pass a `transaction` reference so that Sequelize can execute queries within the lifecycle scopes under the same transaction. We will be covering transactions more in depth in *Chapter 6, Implementing Transactions with Sequelize*, but for now, we will give a simple illustrative example of what a transaction would look like:

```
const Sequelize = require('@sequelize/core');
const sequelize = new Sequelize('db', 'username',
                                'password');
```

```
await sequelize.transaction(async t => {
    // validate our balances here and some other work…

    await Book.create({
        to: 'Joe',
        from: 'Bob',
        amount: 20.21,
    }, {
        transaction: t,
    });

    // double check our new balances
    await checkBalances(t, 'Joe', 'Bob', 20.21);
});
```

The benefit of using a transaction within the lifecycle event is that if any part of the transaction workflow fails to execute, we can halt the rest of the workflow without diluting the quality of our database's records. Without the `transaction` parameter being set within the previous example, Sequelize would still have created a Ledger entry, even if the `checkBalances` method returned an error and did not commit the transaction.

> **Note**
> Sequelize will sometimes use its own internal transaction for methods such as `findOrCreate`. You may always overwrite this parameter with your own transaction.

Now that we have the fundamentals of adding lifecycle events to our models, we can begin updating our Avalon Airlines project.

Putting it all together

For this section, we will only need to update the `BoardingTicket` model (located in `models/boardingticket.js`) by adding two attributes, `cost` and `isEmployee`, and some lifecycle events for our boarding seat workflow. Let's look at the steps:

1. First, we will need to add our attributes within the `init` method, which should end up looking like this:

    ```
    BoardingTicket.init({
        seat: {
    ```

```
      type: DataTypes.STRING,
      validate: {
        notEmpty: {
    msg: 'Please enter in a valid seating arrangement'
        }
      }
    },
    cost: {
      type: DataTypes.DECIMAL(7, 2)
    },
    isEmployee: {
      type: DataTypes.VIRTUAL,
      async get() {
        const customer = await this.getCustomer();
        if (!customer || !customer.email)
            return false;

  return customer.email.endsWith('avalonairlines');
      }
    }
  }, {
    sequelize,
    modelName: 'BoardingTicket'
  });
```

2. Below the `init` function, we will want to add our lifecycle events. The first one will check whether the ticket is considered to be an employee ticket and, if so, then mark the subtotal as zero:

```
// Employees should be able to fly for free
BoardingTicket.beforeValidate('checkEmployee',
                              (ticket, options) => {
  if (ticket.isEmployee) {
    ticket.subtotal = 0;
  }
});
```

3. Next, we will want to ensure our subtotal is never less than zero (the `beforeValidate` event would also be applicable here):

```
// Subtotal should never be less than zero
BoardingTicket.beforeSave('checkSubtotal', (ticket,
options) => {
    if (ticket.subtotal < 0) {
        throw new Error('Invalid subtotal for this
ticket.');
    }
});
```

4. For the last lifecycle event for our model, we will want to check whether the customer had selected a seat that was considered available:

```
// Ensure that the seat the customer has requested
    is available
BoardingTicket.beforeSave('checkSeat', async (tick
                            et, options) => {
// getDataValue will retrieve the new value (as
    opposed to the previous/current value)
const newSeat = ticket.getDataValue('seat');

    if (ticket.changed('seat')) {
      const boardingTicketExists =
      BoardingTick-et.findOne({
        where: { seat: newSeat }
      });

      if (boardingTicketExists) {
        throw new Error(`The seat ${newSeat} has
        al-ready been taken.`)
      }
    }
});
```

5. After these changes, whenever we create a new boarding ticket, our application will now perform three lifecycle events prior to saving the record. For reference only, the following is an example of how we would pass the transaction to our `BoardingTicket` model:

```
await sequelize.transaction(async t => {
  await BookingTicket.create({
    seat: 'A1',
    cost: 12,
    customerId: 1,
  }, {
    transaction: t,
  });
});
```

That wraps up our required changes in this chapter for the Avalon Airlines project. We added a lifecycle event that checks for subtotals and seat availability. We also went through an example of passing a transaction to a specific query, which we will expand upon in the next chapter.

Summary

In this chapter, we went through what a lifecycle event is and how it can be used in day-to-day applications, which lifecycle events are available to Sequelize and in which order they are initiated, and how to add lifecycle events to or remove them from a Sequelize model.

In the next chapter, we will be covering how transactions work, how they are used, and how they can be configured within Sequelize. In addition, the following chapter will also cover different types of locks for transactions and the differences between managed and unmanaged transactions.

References

If you run into issues with lifecycle events, a quick reference can be found here: `https://sequelize.org/master/manual/hooks.html`.

Implementing Transactions with Sequelize

Throughout the previous chapters, we went over how to ensure that data integrity is maintained from within our Node.js application using life cycle events, validations, and constraints. However, these methods do not guarantee that the data is internally consistent in the database itself. Databases offer a way to atomicize integrity using **transactions**.

Transactions are used for ensuring a process has been completed without interruptions such as a connection failure or the power abruptly failing. They are also used for isolating, or locking, applications from manipulating data concurrently, which alleviates **race condition** issues. Transactions promise data validity by following the **ACID** principle, which stands for **atomic** ("all-or-nothing" behavior), **consistent** (adheres to constraints), **isolated** (transactions happen sequentially and unbeknownst toward each other), and **durable** (persistent storage).

A generic use case for transactions would be transferring funds from one user account to another. If *User A* had 30 coins in their account and was charged 20 coins by *User B* just before *User A* decided to make a purchase from another user for 15 coins, then the database should prevent *User A* from being able to purchase the item that costs 15 coins due to a low balance. The database would see that *User A* was charged 20 coins prior to charging 15 coins and then would issue a **rollback** for the second transaction.

> **Note**
> Transactions also offer a feature called **savepoints** that would act as "snapshots of time for the database" with changes made from the transaction itself, which is useful for multi-step transactions. For instance, in a bank scenario, we only transact the currency itself, but in a vendor's shop, we would have to ensure the item and currencies are in their appropriate places.

By default, Sequelize does not execute queries under a transaction, but it does offer two methods for interacting with transactions that are referred to as managed and unmanaged transactions. Managed transactions will either commit the changes or roll back their changes automatically/implicitly depending on whether there is an error. Unmanaged transactions rely on the developer to invoke the appropriate methods for committing or rolling back changes.

In this chapter, we will cover the following areas:

- A more in-depth look at – and examples of—managed and unmanaged transactions
- Using **Continuation-Local Storage (CLS)** for partial transactions
- Managing and configuring advanced transaction options including isolation levels
- Using life cycle events and locks with transactions

Specifically, we will look at the following topics:

- Managed and unmanaged transactions
- Running transactions concurrently
- Isolation levels and advanced configuration
- Putting it all together

> **Note**
> You can always reference Sequelize's code base to maintain an up-to-date list of available transaction methods here:
> `https://github.com/sequelize/sequelize/blob/v6/src/transaction.js`

Technical requirements

You can find the code files of this chapter at `https://github.com/PacktPublishing/Supercharging-Node.js-Application-with-Sequelize/blob/main/ch6`.

Managed and unmanaged transactions

Managed transactions are typically easier for developers with previous **object-relational mapping (ORM)** experience, and unmanaged transactions may be more familiar to developers who write **Structured Query Language (SQL)** directly. Unmanaged transactions are explicit by design, but managed transactions have some implicit behaviors for state management such as automatically creating a transaction instance and calling your callback method with that transaction.

Let's look at the steps for creating unmanaged transactions, as follows:

1. We would start by creating a transaction instance, like so:

```
const tx = await sequelize.transaction();
```

2. Next, we will want to wrap our queries in a `try` block. For this example, we will increment and decrement two account balances by `100` using the same transaction instance, like so:

```
try {
    const amount = 100;

    await Account.increment(
        { balance: amount * -1 },
        {
            where: { id: 1 },
            transaction: tx
        }
    );

    await Account.increment(
        { balance: amount },
        {
            where: { id: 2 },
            transaction: tx
        }
    );
```

The following line of code will commit our transaction if our previous two queries are executed successfully:

```
await tx.commit();
```

3. Now, we can close the `try` block and add a `catch` block for handling any errors thrown from our transaction, as follows:

```
} catch (error) {

    await tx.rollback();
    // log the error here
}
```

The `tx.rollback()` command will tell the database to revert any changes made within this transaction. You may roll back a transaction at any time regardless of whether there is a conditional statement or for error handling.

Sequelize can automate a lot of this work for you by using *managed transactions*. Let us presume that our `Account` model has a constraint where the balance had to be greater than zero, and the sender account only had five coins in its balance. We can rewrite our previous unmanaged transaction example into a managed transaction, like so:

```
try {
    const amount = 100;

    await sequelize.transaction(async (tx) => {
        await Account.increment(
            { balance: amount },
            {
                where: { id: 1 },
                transaction: tx
            }
        );

        await Account.increment(
            { balance: amount * -1 },
            {
                where: { id: 2 },
                transaction: tx
            }
        );
    });

    // the transaction has automatically been committed
} catch (error) {
    // Sequelize has already rolled back the transaction
    from the try block
}
```

Managed transactions will automatically commit or roll back depending on whether an exception was thrown from an applicable query. You can still roll back manually within a managed transaction by throwing an error within the transaction block, as follows:

```
try {
    await sequelize.transaction(async (tx) => {
        // some queries
        throw new Error("rolling back the transaction manu
                        ally here");
        // some more queries
    });
} catch (error) {
    // rolling back the transaction manually here
}
```

Sometimes, our application will require different transactions to run concurrently. We can chain multiple transactions recursively or we could use a module called CLS. In the next section, we will cover how to use concurrent transactions with both methods.

Running transactions concurrently

Depending on whether your application requires isolation between reads and writes, within the database, you may need to explicitly run multiple transactions at the same time. Sequelize offers two methods for running transactions concurrently: recursively chaining transactions (Sequelize's native method) or integrating your application with a third-party module called CLS.

> **Note**
>
> SQLite does not support running multiple transactions concurrently.

Running transactions concurrently with Sequelize

We can run transactions concurrently with Sequelize concurrently by chaining two transaction methods together, which would look similar to this:

```
sequelize.transaction((tx1) => {
    return sequelize.transaction((tx2) => {
```

Now, we can run multiple queries simultaneously while using different transactions, as follows:

```
        return Promise.all([
            Account.create({ id: 1 }, { transaction: null }),
            Account.create({ id: 2 }, { transaction: tx1 }),
            Account.create({ id: 3 }, { transaction: tx2 }),
        ]);
    });
});
```

By default, Sequelize will not use a transaction instance variable. If we were to omit the
`{ transaction: tx2 }` option for the last `Account.create` command, then Sequelize
would not use a transaction instance variable and would act like the first `Account.create`
command with `{ transaction: null }`.

Running transactions with CLS

Using CLS with Sequelize will help you automatically pass transactions to all queries, as well as provide
something similar to thread-local storage. The advantage of CLS' automatic transaction execution is
that some database pool drivers require us to commit transactions across the wire, which would be
cumbersome to manage manually. The thread-local storage gives us the ability to share context across
transactions created in separate parts within our application.

> **Note**
>
> To learn more about CLS, refer to the project's Git repository at `https://github.com/`
> `othiym23/node-continuation-local-storage`.

This book does not integrate CLS with Sequelize, but for completeness, we will cover how to enable
CLS with Sequelize for your project. We will need to install the necessary package, as follows:

```
npm install continuation-local-storage
```

Then, we can initialize a CLS namespace, like so:

```
const cls = require('continuation-local-storage');
const namespace = cls.createNamespace('custom-sequelize-
namespace');
```

We can then pass the `namespace` variable to the Sequelize constructor's `useCLS` method, like so:

```
const Sequelize = require('@sequelize/core');
Sequelize.useCLS(namespace);
const sequelize = new Sequelize(/* … */);
```

Since we are using Sequelize's constructor, all of Sequelize's instances will share the same namespace. Individual CLS instances are not supported by Sequelize at this time.

Borrowing from the previous section's example, we omit to classify the transaction parameter within our queries, as highlighted in the following example:

```
sequelize.transaction((tx1) => {
    return sequelize.transaction((tx2) => {
        return Promise.all([
            Account.create({ id: 1 }, { transaction: null }),
            Account.create({ id: 2 }, { transaction: tx1 }),
            Account.create({ id: 3 }),
        ]);
    });
});
```

With CLS, Sequelize will pass the innermost scoped transaction instance variable, which would be `tx2` from the previous example. If we were to omit the `{ transaction: null }` option for the first `Account.create` command, then Sequelize will presumptuously use `tx2` for its transaction, as in the last `Account.create` command. The second—or middle—`Account.create` command would still explicitly use the `tx1` transaction instance.

Since Sequelize automatically passes a transaction to queries, the following two examples would execute with the same `tx` instance variable:

```
await sequelize.transaction(async () => { // the tx
argument is not required
        await removeUserInventory(id);
        await User.destroy({ where: { id } }); // tx is also
        used here
});
async function removeUserInventory(id) {
    // this query will also use the same scope tx variable
        as User.destroy
```

```
        await UserInventory.destroy({ where: { userId: id } });
}
```

As you can see, enabling CLS with Sequelize can offer some advantages and organize the project's code base a bit better.

> **Note**
>
> For even more functionality with CLS, refer to a project called CLS-Hooked:
>
> `https://github.com/jeff-lewis/cls-hooked`

Isolation levels and advanced configuration

In this section, we will be covering the different isolation levels and configuration options available from Sequelize for every type of transaction. For managed transactions, the method signature looks like this: `sequelize.transaction(options, callback)`. The unmanaged transaction signature is `sequelize.transaction(options)`.

Here is a list of configurable options for both transaction types:

- `type`—A SQLite option to set the transaction type. Possible values are `DEFERRED` (the default), `IMMEDIATE`, and `EXCLUSIVE`. Refer to `https://www.sqlite.org/lang_transaction.html`.

- `isolationLevel`—Sets the transaction's isolation level. The following explanations are under the context of MySQL but should be applicable to other **database management systems (DBMS)** with minute differences. There are four available levels for Sequelize, as outlined here:

  - `READ_UNCOMMITTED`—Reads data using non-locking mechanisms. This could cause concurrency issues using stale, or invalid, data from other transactions that have been rolled back.

  - `READ_COMMITTED`—Performs consistent reads even from within the same transaction. In other words, reading data will be consistent with updates performed from prior queries within the same transaction.

  - `REPEATABLE_READ`—Similar to `READ_COMMITTED` when it comes to reading the information, but there are some stipulations when it comes to MySQL's InnoDB database engines explicitly. Refer to `https://dev.mysql.com/doc/refman/5.7/en/innodb-transaction-isolation-levels.html#isolevel_repeatable-read` for more information on how to consistently lock records for when you need to.

  - `SERIALIZABLE`—A stricter ruleset than `REPEATABLE_READ`. This isolation level is generally used for figuring out concurrency and deadlock-related issues for the database.

- `deferrable`—Applicable to PostgreSQL only, this setting determines whether constraints can be deferred or checked immediately.

- `logging`—A function that Sequelize will pass a query and its parameters as arguments.

Sequelize offers constant variables for convenience when setting isolation levels, like so:

```
const Sequelize = require('@sequelize/core');
sequelize.transaction({
    isolationLevel: Sequelize.Transaction.ISOLATION_LEVELS.
                    SERIALIZABLE
}, (tx) => { /* ... */ });
```

We can also set the transaction's isolation level on an instance level by setting the `isolationLevel` option when initializing Sequelize, as follows:

```
new Sequelize('db', 'user', 'pw', {
    isolationLevel: Sequelize.Transaction.ISOLATION_LEVELS.
                    READ_COMMITTED
});
```

Now, any subsequent transactions will use the READ_COMMITTED level by default. These isolation levels pertain to reading data. In the next section, we will go over locking mechanisms for writing data to the database.

Locking rows with Sequelize

Sometimes, our application requires us to temporarily lock information while performing a transaction and prevent other transactions from committing to the same table or row. Database practitioners may know this mechanism as a SELECT FOR UPDATE query. You can see an example of such a query in the following code snippet:

```
sequelize.transaction((tx) => {
    const seat = Seats.findOne({
        where: { venue: 1, row: 5, seat: 13 }
        transaction: tx,
        lock: true
    });
    // ... more queries ...
});
```

Presuming that each `row` and `seat` instance is unique per `venue` instance, the previous example will lock that particular seat's record until the transaction has been committed or rolled back.

Suppose we wanted to retrieve a list of seats that were not in a pending transaction. If our DBMS supports the `SKIP LOCKED` command, then we can use a `skipLocked: true` configuration option when querying data. To demonstrate the `SKIP LOCKED` feature, we can begin by adding a locked record for a particular seat, as follows:

```
const tx1 = await sequelize.transaction();
const seat = Seats.findOne({
    where: { venue: 1, row: 5, seat: 13 }
    transaction: tx1,
    lock: true
});
```

Next, the following query will use the `SKIP LOCKED` rule and return any applicable row that is not locked by another pending transaction (in this particular case, row 5, seat 13):

```
const tx2 = await sequelize.transaction();

const seats = Seats.findAll({
    where: { venue: 1 }
    transaction: tx2,
    lock: true,
    skipLocked: true
});
```

> **Note**
>
> MySQL added support for `SKIP LOCKED` from version 8.0.1. This book's code base will not require `skipLocked`, but if you are using an older version and try to use `skipLocked`, then Sequelize will silently omit the `SKIP LOCKED` command from the query and may yield unexpected behaviors or results.

Using life cycle events for transactions

Sequelize only offers one life cycle—even for transactions—explicitly at the moment. This life cycle event, named `afterCommit`, can be used for both managed and unmanaged transactions. This event will not be triggered if the transaction gets rolled back, nor can the event modify its transaction object (unlike traditional life cycle events).

To invoke the `afterCommit` hook, we can add the event to the transaction's instance, like so:

```
sequelize.transaction((tx) => {
    tx.afterCommit((trx) => {
        // … your logic here ...
    });


    // ... queries using tx ...
});
```

We can append `afterCommit` events to an entire model via the `afterSave` event. A good use case for using `afterCommit` is sending serialized data to some other service, application, blockchain database, and so on. Here is an example of how to use `afterCommit`:

```
Seats.afterSave((instance, options) => {
    if (options.transaction) {
        // appending afterCommit to the transaction instance
here
        options.transaction.afterCommit(() => { /* your logic
here */ });
        return;
    }
    // code will continue here if we did not save under a
transaction
});
```

So far, we have gone over the different kinds of transactions that Sequelize offers, namespace environments for transactions, isolation levels, locking, and life cycle events. Using a combination of these skillsets, we can finally start implementing some of this knowledge into our application.

Putting it all together

Now that we have gone over the core tenets of using transactions with Sequelize, we can begin adding to our *Avalon Airlines* project. Our business partner just informed us that the investors want a small demonstration for booking a flight without processing a payment. For this task, we will need to add a couple of new files, update the `BoardingTicket` and `FlightSchedule` models, add new routes to our express application, and install a new Node.js package.

First, let us begin by adding the new Node.js package that the project will require. This package is known as Luxon (https://moment.github.io/luxon/), which is a date-and-time JavaScript library. Use the following command to add the package:

```
npm i --save luxon
```

Next, we will want to modify a life cycle event that exists within the `BoardingTicket` model located in `models/boardingticket.js` by adding/changing the following highlighted code:

```
BoardingTicket.beforeSave('checkSeat', async (ticket, options)
=> {
    const newSeat = ticket.getDataValue('seat');
    const { transaction } = options;

    if (ticket.changed('seat')) {
        const boardingTicketExists = await BoardingTicket.
findOne({
            where: {
                seat: newSeat
            },
            transaction,
        });

        if (boardingTicketExists !== null) {
            throw new Error(`The seat ${newSeat} has already been
taken.`);
        }
    }
});
```

The other model that we will need to add a few updates to is the `FlightSchedule` model located in `models/flightschedule.js`. Add the following line of code to the top of the file:

```
const { DateTime } = require('luxon');
```

After that, add another validation within the `validate` object just below the `validDestination` method, as follows:

```
validateDepartureTime() {
    const dt = DateTime.fromJSDate(this.departureTime);
```

```
      if (!dt.isValid) {
        throw new Error("Invalid departure time");
      }

      if (dt < DateTime.now()) {
        throw new Error("The departure time must be set
                        within the future");
      }
    },
```

Now, we can add a new folder and file located at `routes/flights.js` from the project's main directory and add the following lines of code to load the appropriate modules and files:

```
const { DateTime } = require("luxon");
const models = require("../models");
```

For our first flight-related route, we will need to find a way to create our airplanes first. Looking at the attributes from `models/airplane.js`, we can determine that we will need a model name and the number of seats for each airplane. The code is illustrated in the following code snippet:

```
async function createAirplane(req, res) {
    const { name, seats } = req.body;
```

Within the POST data, we will expect name and `seats` values to be sent to our Express application. Now, we can add the airplane creation logic, along with closing and exporting the function, as follows:

```
    try {
        const airplane = await models.Airplane.create({
            planeModel: name,
            totalSeats: seats,
        });

        return res.json(airplane);
    } catch (error) {
        res.status(500).send(error);
    }
}
exports.createAirplane = createAirplane;
```

Our next function will be for creating flight schedules. We will require `airplaneId`, `origin`, `destination`, and `departure` POST values for creating flight schedules, as follows:

```
async function createSchedule(req, res) {
    const { airplaneId, origin, destination, departure } =
    req.body;
```

First, let us validate and parse the departure time into a native `DateTime` object, like so:

```
const dt = DateTime.fromISO(departure);
if (!dt.isValid) {
    return res.status(400).send("invalid departure
                                    time");
}
```

Next, we will want to check whether the airplane actually exists, so we'll execute the following code to find out:

```
try {
const plane = await models.Airplane.findByPk(airplaneId);
    if (!plane) {
        return res.status(404).send("airplane does not
                                    exist");
    }
}
```

If the airplane does exist, we will want to create a flight schedule for it. We will wrap the creation in a transaction to ensure that creating the schedule, and associating the schedule with a particular airplane, would yield no errors.

For this particular demonstration, a transaction is not necessary, but in a real-world application, we would want to make sure that an airplane is not overbooked based on routing and departing times. The transaction block would look like this:

```
const flight = await sequelize.transaction(async
(tx) => {
const schedule = await models.FlightSchedule.create({
        originAirport: origin,
        destinationAirport: destination,
        departureTime: dt,
    }, { transaction: tx });
```

We follow this by setting the associated airplane, returning the schedule record, finishing the transaction, and rendering a response with **JavaScript Object Notation (JSON)** data, like so:

```
        await schedule.setAirplane(plane,
        { transaction: tx });
        return schedule;
    });
    return res.json(flight);
```

The last part of this file is capturing any errors from the previous `try` block and exporting the `createSchedule` function, like so:

```
    } catch (error) {
        return res.status(500).send(error);
    }
}
exports.createSchedule = createSchedule;
```

Now, we can create a new file located at `routes/tickets.js` that will serve as the route for booking our actual flight. For demonstration purposes, we will omit complex functionalities such as determining prices and customer sessions and fill in those details with constant values. After creating the file, we would load our models at the top of the file, as follows:

```
const models = require("../models");
```

For our `bookTicket` method, we will need a `scheduleId` and `seat` POST parameter, in addition to opening a transaction for creating a ticket. Here's how we can add these:

```
async function bookTicket(req, res) {
    try {
        const { scheduleId, seat } = req.body;

        const t = await sequelize.transaction(async (tx) => {
```

Check to see whether the `FlightSchedule` model exists by executing the following code:

```
const schedule = await models.FlightSchedule.findByPk
(scheduleId, {transaction: tx});
            if (!schedule) {
                throw new Error("schedule could not be
```

```
                                              found");
          }
```

Let's create our new boarding ticket, like so:

```
const boardingTicket = await models.BoardingTicket.create({
                seat,
        }, { transaction: tx });
```

We'll now set our boarding ticket's associations and then return the ticket while completing the transaction, as follows:

```
                // this is where we would set a customer if we had
an application with authentication, etc.
                // await ticket.setCustomer(customerId, {
transaction: tx });
                await schedule.addBoardingTicket(boardingTicket, {
transaction: tx });

                return boardingTicket;
        });

        return res.json(t.toJSON());
```

Capture any errors and export the function, like so:

```
        } catch (error) {
                return res.status(400).send(error.toString());
        }
}
exports.bookTicket = bookTicket;
```

Next, we will want to add a module called `body-parser` that helps transform different **Hypertext Transfer Protocol** (**HTTP**) post encoding content types (with the exception of multipart) into JavaScript objects and notation (passed down as `req.body` in Express). For more information, visit `https://github.com/expressjs/body-parser`. We can install and add the package to our `package.json` file with the following command:

```
npm i --save body-parser
```

Our last file to edit would be the `index.js` file within the project's main directory. We will want to add the following module after requiring the express module on the first line:

```
const bodyParser = require("body-parser");
```

Just below the `const models = require("./models");` line, we will want to add our new exported functions. Here's how we do this:

```
const { bookTicket } = require("./routes/tickets")
const { createAirplane, createSchedule } = require("./routes/
flights");
```

Just above the first route, `app.get('/', …)`, add the following line of code for JSON POST support:

```
app.use(bodyParser.json({ type: 'application/json' }));
```

Next, we will want to add the following line of code above the `app.get('/airplanes/:id', ...)` line for our `createAirplane` route:

```
app.post('/airplanes', createAirplane);
```

Then, we can add our remaining new routes just above the `app.listen(3000, ...)` line, like so:

```
app.post('/schedules', createSchedule);
app.post('/book-flight', bookTicket);
```

Since all of our changes have been committed, we can now run our application by executing the following command:

```
npm run start
```

In order to test our application, we can use cURL or any HTTP REST utility such as Postman (https://www.postman.com/) or HTTPie (https://httpie.io/). Let us create a new airplane before a flight schedule, as follows:

```
curl -X POST -H "Content-Type: application/json" -d "{\"name\":
\"A320\", \"seats\": -1}" http://127.0.0.1:3000/airplanes
```

We should see a response similar to this:

```
{"name":"SequelizeValidationError","errors":[{"message":"A
plane must have at least one seat","type":"Validation error","p
ath":"totalSeats","value":-1,"origin":"FUNCTION","instance":{"i
d":null,"planeModel":"A320","totalSeats":-1,"updatedAt":"2022-
02-21T16:27:18.336Z","createdAt":"2022-02-21T16:27:18.336Z"},"v
```

```
alidatorKey":"min","validatorName":"min","validatorArgs":[1],"o
riginal":{"validatorName":"min","validatorArgs":[1]}}]}
```

This particular A320 model has up to 150 seats available at a time for customers. When we adjust our total number of seats available, our new command would look like this:

```
curl -X POST -H "Content-Type: application/json" -d "{\"name\":
\"A320\", \"seats\": 150}" http://127.0.0.1:3000/airplanes
```

The preceding command should return a response similar to this:

```
{"id":1,"planeModel":"A320","totalSeats":150,"updatedAt":"2022-
02-21T15:49:19.883Z","createdAt":"2022-02-21T15:49:19.883Z"}
```

We will want to keep the id value in mind for the next command when creating a schedule:

```
curl -X POST -H "Content-Type: application/
json" -d "{\"airplaneId\": 1, \"origin\":
\"LAX\", \"destination\": \"ORD\", \"departure\":
\"2060-01-01T14:00:00Z\"}"  http://127.0.0.1:3000/schedules
```

The preceding request should result in an error that looks similar to this:

```
{"name":"SequelizeValidationError","errors":[{"message":
"Invalid destination airport","type":"Validation error","path":
"destinationAirport","value":"ORD","origin":"LAX","instance":{
"id":null,"originAirport":"LAX","destinationAirport":"ORD",
"updatedAt":"2022-02-21T18:11:02.108Z","createdAt":"2022-02-
21T18:11:02.108Z"},"validatorKey":"isIn","validatorName":
"isIn","validatorArgs":[["MIA","JFK","LAX"]],"original":
{"validatorName":"isIn","validatorArgs":[["MIA","JFK","LAX"]]
}}]}
```

We currently do not fly to Chicago's O'Hare International Airport! The new destination will now be Miami using the MIA code, as illustrated here:

```
curl -X POST -H "Content-Type: application/json" -d
"{\"airplaneId\": 1, \"origin\": \"LAX\", \"destination\":
\"MIA\", \"departure\": \"2060-01-01T14:00:00Z\"}"
http://127.0.0.1:3000/schedules
```

The response should look similar to this:

```
{"id":1,"originAirport":"LAX","destinationAirport"
:"MIA","departureTime":"2060-01-01T14:00:00.000Z",
"updatedAt":"2022-02-21T18:34:46.049Z","createdAt"-
:"2022-02-21T18:34:46.038Z","AirplaneId":1}
```

For the booking request, we will need the previous response's id value and a seating assignment, as follows:

```
curl -X POST -H "Content-Type: application/json" -d
"{\"scheduleId\": 1, \"seat\": \"1A\"}" http://127.0.0.1:3000/
book-flight
```

The response would look similar to this:

```
{"isEmployee":{},"id":1,"seat":"1A","updatedAt":"2022-02-21T18:
55:30.837Z","createdAt":"2022-02-21T18:55:30.837Z"}
```

If we were to repeat the previous command, an error message would be shown to us indicating that the seat has already been taken, as shown here:

```
Error: The seat 1A has already been taken.
```

That wraps up our changes to the *Avalon Airlines* project. We implemented a way to create airplanes and new flight schedules and assign boarding tickets with transactions. This should complete the requirements for our next investor meeting.

Summary

In this chapter, we went through the differences between managed and unmanaged transactions, using CLS for global scoping transactions, the supported isolation levels, applicable life cycle events, and locking transactions.

In the next chapter, we will be covering how to handle customized, JSON, and **binary large object** (**BLOB**) data directly from Sequelize to the DBMS. The following chapter will also contain further instructions on completing the *Avalon Airlines* project.

7
Handling Customized, JSON, and Blob Data Types

Some database management systems offer a way of storing niche column types such as JSON and Blob-related data. These column types are useful for rapid prototyping, handling schemaless data, and sending and receiving buffered data.

Typically, an application would use a **NoSQL** database, such as MongoDB, to process and query JSON documents, but this comes with a set of its own problems. We can no longer adhere to some sort of normalization for our structures without an extensive list of validations, and the NoSQL database cannot perform transactions nor provide ACID-compliant capabilities.

> **Note**
> Some NoSQL databases claim to offer ACID compliance, but they often come with stipulations and limitations such as a maximum number of documents that can be updated in a single transaction, or a transaction cannot take longer than some temporal window; otherwise, you will lose all of the performance advantages of NoSQL over SQL databases.

There are several use cases for JSON and Blob column data types. With JSON, you can store a record set of non-deterministic values, which is great for use cases such as creating receipts of transactions and auditing systems. A Blob column data type can store any file that helps centralize retrieving and inserting from one location, but internally, the DBMS could shard or distribute that file.

Usually, it is not recommended to store files within a DBMS due to losing external access control lists, clogging Write-Ahead log files, and a false sense of security for storing those files. We could also run into increased page sizes, which would increase the time it takes to retrieve records. As a general rule, for quick prototyping of handling files, using a DBMS is fine but not for a production environment.

> **Note**
> An example of using a JSON column type for auditing would be PGAudit's Postgres extension. This extension will convert the previous and new record sets as JSON data types for storing differentiating values. You may refer to `https://www.pgaudit.org/` for more information on how this works.

Sequelize is capable of handling custom and Blob types for all supported DBMSs, and JSON column types for SQLite, MySQL, MariaDB, and PostgreSQL only. There is a workaround for MSSQL, which will be explained in detail under the *Working with JSON* section of this chapter.

In this chapter, we will cover the following:

- Querying JSON and JSONB data
- Using the BLOB column type
- Creating custom data types

Technical requirements

You can find the code files of this chapter at `https://github.com/PacktPublishing/Supercharging-Node.js-Application-with-Sequelize/blob/main/ch7`.

Querying JSON and JSONB data

As stated previously, JSON column types are only available for SQLite, MySQL, MariaDB, and PostgreSQL. The JSONB column is only supported on the PostgreSQL DBMS. The difference between the two column types is that JSONB will store additional information related to the fields within the JSON document internally. This will increase the requirements for disk space but will help make querying the data quicker.

For this section, presume that we have the following model within our application:

```
class Receipts extends Model {}
Receipts.init({
  receipt: DataTypes.JSON
});
```

Now, we can create our document:

```
await Receipts.create({
    receipt: {
        name: {
```

```
                first: "Bob",
                last: "Smith"
            },
            items: [
                {
                    sku: "abc123",
                    quantity: 10
                },
                {
                    sku: "xyz321",
                    quantity: 1
                }
            ],
            subtotal: 100
        }
});
```

We can now query for our document using the traditional Sequelize methods:

```
await Receipts.findOne({
    where: {
        receipt: {
            name: {
                first: "Bob",
                last: "Smith"
            }
        }
    }
});
```

Or we can use a special dot-notation style:

```
await Receipts.findOne({
    where: {
        "receipts.name.first": "Bob",
        "receipts.name.last": "Smith"
    }
});
```

The dot-notation method will also work on other finder attributes such as `order`:

```
const receipts = await Receipts.findAll({
    where: {
      receipt: {
        name: {
          last: "Smith",
        },
      },
    },
    order: [
      ["receipt.name.first"]
    ]
});
```

We would have to re-insert the entire document like traditional NoSQL document storage systems when updating records:

```
await Receipts.update({
    receipt: {
        name: {
            first: "Bob",
            last: "Smith"
        },
        items: [
            {
                sku: "abc123",
                quantity: 10
            },
            {
                sku: "xyz321",
                quantity: 1
            }
        ],
        subtotal: 120
    }
}, {
    where: {
```

```
        "receipt.name.first": "Bob"
    }
});
```

If we wanted to query for a value within an array, we may need to use the `Sequelize.literal` function if our DBMS does not natively support the `Op.contains` operator (PostgreSQL only). The following is an example of how to query an array's value with PostgreSQL's `@>` operator:

```
const receipts = await Receipts.findAll({
    where: {
        receipt: {
            items: {
                [Op.contains]: {
                    sku: "abc123"
                }
            }
        }
    }
});
```

Since MySQL does not support a `contains` operator, the equivalent of the previous query would look like the following:

```
const receipts = await Receipts.findAll({
    where: Sequelize.literal(`JSON_CONTAINS(JSON_EXTRACT
        (receipt, '$.items[*].sku', '"abc123"')`)
});
```

MSSQL can also perform basic operations for JSON. The following is an example of how to query JSON data with MSSQL and Sequelize:

```
class Users extends Model {}
Users.init({
    metadata: DataTypes.STRING
});

await Users.create({
    metadata: JSON.stringify({
        first_name: "Bob",
```

```
        last_name: "Smith"
    })
});


await Users.findAll({
    where: sequelize.where(
        sequelize.fn('JSON_VALUE', sequelize.col('metadata'),
'$.first_name'),
        'Bob'
    )
});
```

Unfortunately for MSSQL, to search through nested arrays would require a cross-join and a few more topics that are out of this book's scope, such as OpenJSON (which can be referenced at `https://docs.microsoft.com/en-us/sql/t-sql/functions/openjson-transact-sql?view=sql-server-ver15`).

Using the BLOB column type

Sometimes, our application will require us to store buffer or binary data in our system. The following is a quick example of how to create and read binary data with Sequelize:

1. We will start with our definition:

```
class Users extends Model {}
Users.init({
    avatar: DataTypes.BLOB,
    keycode: DataTypes.BLOB
});
```

2. Next, we can insert our record, like so:

```
await Users.create({
    avatar: require("fs").readFileSync
            ("/some/path/avatar.jpg"),
    keycode: Buffer.from("secretpassword")
});
```

3. To retrieve and use the buffered data, we can simply use a finder method and write directly using Node.js' `fs` module:

```
const user = await Users.findOne({});

require("fs").writeFileSync(
    "/some/path/to/write/avatar.jpg",
    user.avatar
);
```

Now that we have gone through all of the built-in data types, we can now begin creating our own custom data type. Custom data types can also be useful for just extending several validations together or creating several rulesets into one data type.

Creating custom data types

Sequelize offers us a way to create custom types by extending the `DataTypes.ABSTRACT` abstraction class. This allows us to keep our code base more organized and consistent. Suppose our application required a lot of columns all abiding by the laws of natural numbers. A quick demonstration would look like this:

```
class Stats extends Model {}
Stats.init({
    A: {
        type: Sequelize.INTEGER(11).UNSIGNED.ZEROFILL,
        validate: {
            min: 1
        }
    },
    B: {
        type: Sequelize.INTEGER(11).UNSIGNED.ZEROFILL,
        validate: {
            min: 1
        }
    },
    C: {
        type: Sequelize.INTEGER(11).UNSIGNED.ZEROFILL,
        validate: {
            min: 1
```

```
        }
    },
});
```

If we had hundreds of these columns, writing these columns out could be tiresome. A way to resolve this issue would be to create our own custom attribute. Let's look at the steps:

1. The first step is to extend the `ABSTRACT` class:

    ```
    class NATURAL_NUMBER extends DataTypes.ABSTRACT {
    ```

2. Then, we will need to tell Sequelize how to translate this data type into a column type. We can do this by defining a `toSql` method within the class:

    ```
    toSql() {
        return 'INTEGER(11) UNSIGNED ZEROFILL'
    }
    ```

    This will tell Sequelize that we want a zero-filled and unsigned integer.

3. Next, we can enforce a validation rule by creating a `validate` method:

    ```
    validate(value, options) {
        const isNumber = Number.isInteger(value);
        const isAboveZero = Number.parseInt(value) > 0;

        return isNumber && isAboveZero;
    }
    ```

    Sequelize will automatically check whether the value is an integer and above zero for this attribute type.

4. The next step is optional, but for completeness, the following methods are for writing and reading to and from the database, respectively:

    ```
    _stringify(value) {
      return value.toString();
    }
    static parse(value) {
        return Number.parseInt(value);
    }
    ```

    The `_stringify` method will convert the value into a string before sending it off to your database, and the `parse` method will transform the returned value from the database.

5. Now, we can close our class and invoke some mandatory methods:

```
}

NATURAL_NUMBER.prototype.key = NATURAL_NUMBER.key =
'NATURAL_NUMBER';
DataTypes.NATURAL_NUMBER = Sequelize.Utils.
classToInvokable(NATURAL_NUMBER);
```

Sequelize will identify your attribute's data type by mapping out the key value from your class. The next line will add your custom data type to Sequelize's DataTypes namespace. The classToInvokable method will simply wrap your class's constructor and return a new instance so that you do not have to explicitly call new DataTypes.NATURAL_NUMBER() when defining your models.

6. Now we can define our previous model, like so:

```
class Stats extends Model {}
Stats.init({
    A: DataTypes.NATURAL_NUMBER,
    B: DataTypes.NATURAL_NUMBER,
    C: DataTypes.NATURAL_NUMBER
});
```

And when we go to create or update, our attributes will abide by the rules that we previously set. The following three examples will return a validation error due to the value of the C column not being a natural number:

```
await Stats.create({
    A: 100,
    B: 20,
    C: "NotANumber" // not an number
});

await Stats.create({
    A: 100,
    B: 20,
    C: 1.1 // not an integer
});

await Stats.create({
```

```
    A: 100,
    B: 20,
    C: -3 // not a natural number
});
```

When we change C to a natural number (as shown in the following code), our query will now successfully create the record:

```
await Stats.create({
    A: 100,
    B: 20,
    C: 10
}); // success!
```

So far, we have gone over how to handle JSON and BLOB data types using Sequelize's built-in classes. We also created our own custom data types by extending the Sequelize ABSTRACT data type class. Now, we can start using some of these data types in our project.

Now that we have a better understanding of how to handle JSON data types explicitly, we can start using that type in our Avalon Airlines project.

Putting it all together

Our business partner just informed us that we want to be able to record transaction receipts for every applicable event. This could be for the boarding ticket, extra luggage, or an additional water bottle, which means there is no deterministic structure for our data. For this task, we will need to generate a new model, Receipts, and update our BoardingTicket model. Here are the steps:

1. First, we can begin by generating a new model called Receipts for storing transaction events:

    ```
    sequelize-cli model:generate --name Receipts --attributes
    receipt:json
    ```

2. Then, run our migration:

    ```
    sequelize db:migrate
    ```

3. Next, we will want to add another life cycle event to our BoardingTicket model located in models/boardingticket.js by adding the following code at the end of the module.exports block:

    ```
    BoardingTicket.afterSave('saveReceipt',
        async(ticket, options) => {
    ```

```
        await sequelize.models.Receipts.create({
          receipt: ticket.get()
        }, {
          transaction: options.transaction
        });
    });
```

That wraps up our changes to the Avalon Airlines project. We implemented a new model for storing receipt data using JSON, and we added a life cycle event after creating or updating the `BoardingTicket` model. This should complete the requirements for our next investor meeting.

Summary

In this chapter, we went through different ways of reading and writing attributes with specific data types such as JSON and `BLOB`. We also learned how to create custom data types by extending the `ABSTRACT` class in order to create a more ergonomic code base that is easier to maintain overall.

In the next chapter, we will be covering how to monitor and log queries from your application. The following chapter will also contain further instructions on completing the Avalon Airlines project.

Part 3 –
Advanced Queries, Using Adapters, and Logging Queries

In this part, you will understand how to monitor and measure metrics for your application's performance. You will use third-party applications that integrate with Sequelize and logging queries. You will also learn how to deploy your application to a cloud application platform.

This part comprises the following chapters:

- *Chapter 8, Logging and Monitoring Your Application*
- *Chapter 9, Using and Creating Adapters*
- *Chapter 10, Deploying a Sequelize Application*

8
Logging and Monitoring Your Application

Maintaining records and metrics provides us with many advantages during our development cycle. They can help us increase our application's performance, observe issues before they become problems, and give us insights into the application's state. Logging and monitoring your application can reduce the time your development (and debugging) takes, as well as the number of headaches you acquire throughout the project. Logging is something that is often overlooked or treated with minimal afterthought, but it could make the difference between losing an hour's worth of uptime or an entire day's worth.

Suppose we had an application that simply inserted the details of a registration form into a database table. One day, the team accidentally renamed the `first_name` column to `firstname` and now no new records were being inserted. With logging, we would see something along the lines of a "`first_name` column does not exist" type of error. This would help guide us into looking at the database's schema and figuring out where the disconnection is occurring (in this case, our typo from removing the underscore).

What if the error was more complex than that though? Our application is now running in a cluster and each node within the cluster receives a unique message exclusively from the other nodes. Occasionally, we would notice our table was missing some records without a clear pattern from the data itself. Using a logging mechanism, we would occasionally see a `Could not establish connection` error. We can double-check our connection pooling management (if applicable) or test each node if we can successfully connect to the database. On a small cluster, this would not be a problem, but on a large system, this could become tedious and time-consuming.

A solution for helping manage applications in a larger cluster would be to customize (or add) additional context to your application's logging records. Meta-information such as the machine's identifier could have helped us in the previous example. Sequelize offers a way to customize our logging, using an `options.logging` parameter, with the ability to change the logging behavior with different method invocations.

In this chapter, we will be covering the following topics:

- Configuring logging with all of the available interfaces

- Integrating third-party logging applications such as Pino or Bunyan

- Collecting metrics and statistics for Sequelize with OpenTelemetry

Technical requirements

You can find the code files for this chapter at `https://github.com/PacktPublishing/` `Supercharging-Node.js-Applications-with-Sequelize/tree/main/ch8`

Configuring logging with all of the available interfaces

Sequelize offers a few overload signatures for incorporating logs into an application. The default behavior is to call `console.log` for each query. The following is a list of signatures that Sequelize will abide by:

- `function (msg) {}`

- `function (...msg) {}`

- `true/false`

- `msg => someLogger.debug(msg)`

- `someLogger.debug.bind(someLogger)`

If we wanted to customize Sequelize's logging behavior, the following example would be a quick introduction to how to do so:

```
function customLog(msg) {
    // insert into db/logger app here
    // ...
    // and output to stdout
    console.log(msg);
}

const sequelize = new Sequelize('sqlite::memory:', {
    logging: customLog
});
```

In addition to Sequelize sending the SQL queries into our customLog function, we are also given a helper method for when we need to log additional info beyond our queries. The Sequelize instance provides a log method and can be called as shown here:

```
sequelize.log('this will send our message to customLog as
well');
```

If your Sequelize instance's benchmark parameter is set to true, then Sequelize will add the total elapsed time for the query to complete at the end of the message. Using our previous example, a log entry might look something similar to this:

Executed (default): SELECT * FROM ...; Elapsed time: 136ms

Sometimes, we will want to log the log query, query objects, applicable parameters, or any other form of metadata. Sequelize will recognize the spread pattern for this type of support:

```
function multiLog(...msgs) {
    msgs.forEach(function(msg) {
        console.log(msg);
    });
}


const sequelize = new Sequelize('sqlite::memory:', {
    logging: multiLog
});
```

We can now call the Sequelize instance's log method, which will send the parameters to our multiLog function as follows:

```
sequelize.log('error', 'custom error message', Date.now(), {
id: 100 });
```

This would print each parameter onto its own newline due to the behavior of the multiLog function.

The logging parameter can also accept a Boolean value. The true value will coalesce into Sequelize's default behavior (console.log). Setting the value to false would disable logging completely and nullify any log invocations. The following example would prevent Sequelize from logging queries:

```
const sequelize = new Sequelize('sqlite::memory:', {
    logging: false
});
```

> **Note**
> The `true` value for logging is considered deprecated and is not preferable to omitting the logging value for the default behavior or using `console.log` as the parameter's value.

Sequelize can also limit logging to specific queries with the logging parameter on each queryable method (for example, `findAll`, `update`, and `create`). For instance, if we wanted to disable logging on a specific query, we can do so by setting the following query's `logging` parameter to `false`:

```
sequelize.findAll({
  where: {
    id: 1
  }
}, {
  logging: false
});
```

> **Note**
> You can also see a log output of queries by taking advantage of Sequelize's use of the debug NPM package. By setting the environment variable to `DEBUG=sequelize:sql*`, your terminal should show queries executed by Sequelize.

Integrating third-party logging applications such as Pino or Bunyan

If our application already utilizes a third-party application for logging, Sequelize can offer support for integrating with such systems. This section references two logging applications, Pino and Bunyan, but any logging library or framework should also be compatible with Sequelize.

Integrating with Pino

Pino is a low overhead Node.js logger that also offers redaction, transport, and asynchronous support. Presuming our project has Pino installed within our `node_modules` folder, we can simply integrate it with our Sequelize instance as follows:

```
const logger = require('pino')();
const sequelize = new Sequelize('sqlite::memory:', {
    logging: (msg) => logger.debug(msg)
});
```

Integrating third-party logging applications such as Pino or Bunyan   181

Now, when we call `sequelize.log` manually or execute queries, the logs will be sent to the Pino logging library. The output would look similar to this:

```
{"level":30,"time":1650118644700,"pid":5363,"hostname":"MacB
ook-Pro-4.local","msg":"Executing (default): SHOW INDEX FROM
`Airplanes` FROM `airline`"}
```

For more information on Pino, you can refer to the project's repository at `https://github.com/pinojs/pino`.

Integrating with Bunyan

Sometimes a logging framework requires an intermediary step before being able to bind the framework to Sequelize. An example of this would be the Bunyan framework. Bunyan is a logging framework that focuses on offering serialization and streaming methods. Integrating this framework would look similar to the following:

```
const bunyan = require('bunyan');
const logger = bunyan.createLogger({name: 'app'});

const sequelize = new Sequelize('sqlite::memory:', {
    logging: (msg) => logger.info(msg)
});
```

The preceding example shows the output of Bunyan's logging with Sequelize:

```
{"name":"app","hostname":"MacBook-Pro-4.
local","pid":6014,"level":30,"msg":"Executing (default):
SHOW INDEX FROM `Airplanes` FROM `airline`","time":"2022-04-
16T14:33:13.083Z","v":0}
```

For more information on Bunyan, you can refer to the project's repository at `https://github.com/trentm/node-bunyan`.

From the Pino and Bunyan examples, we can see that adding a logging framework already resolves our unique machine identifier, the time of the error, and urgency research. By looking at the logs, it should now be easier to sift through wherever an error is occurring within clusters or applications.

We can now finish integrating a logging framework within the Avalon Airlines project. From the project's root directory, we will need to install the necessary package:

```
npm i pino
```

Within `models/index.js`, see the following line:

```
const Sequelize = require('sequelize/core');
```

Export the Pino framework underneath with a constant:

```
const logger = require('pino')();
```

After exporting the constant, see this line:

```
const db = {};
```

Underneath, we can add the logging parameter to the `config` object as follows:

```
config.logging = (msg) => logger.info(msg);
```

Now, our application supports custom logs using the Pino logging framework.

Collecting metrics and statistics for Sequelize with OpenTelemetry

OpenTelemetry is a standardized specification for collecting, aggregating, and instrumenting various statistics, metrics, traces, and logs. OpenTelemetry can help us identify where bottlenecks may occur, categorize and apply topological filters on logs, and plug into third-party applications (for example, for alert monitoring).

To integrate OpenTelemetry with Sequelize, we would need to install the following packages within our Avalon Airlines project:

```
npm i @opentelemetry/api @opentelemetry/sdk-trace-node @
opentelemetry/instrumentation @opentelemetry/sdk-node @
opentelemetry/auto-instrumentations-node opentelemetry-
instrumentation-sequelize
```

Within `models/index.js`, under the `'use strict';` line, we can now add our new packages:

```
const { NodeTracerProvider } =
    require('@opentelemetry/sdk-trace-node');
const { registerInstrumentations } =
    require('@opentelemetry/instrumentation');
const { SequelizeInstrumentation } =
    require('opentelemetry-instrumentation-sequelize');
```

Just above the `let sequelize;` line, we can add the trace provider, which will register the correct Sequelize OpenTelemetry plugin:

```
const tracerProvider = new NodeTracerProvider({
  plugins: {
    sequelize: {
      // disabling the default/old plugin is required
      enabled: false,
      path: <opentelemetry-plugin-sequelize'
    }
  }
});
```

Below the `traceProvider` declaration block, we can associate the provider with the Sequelize instrument specifications:

```
registerInstrumentations({
  tracerProvider,
  instrumentations: [
    new SequelizeInstrumentation({
      // any custom instrument options here
    })
  ]
});
```

> **Note**
>
> You can find additional references and option parameters for Sequelize instrumentation at `https://github.com/aspecto-io/opentelemetry-ext-js/tree/master/packages/instrumentation-sequelize`.

At the root directory of the Avalon Airlines project, create a file called `tracing.js` with the following code:

```
const opentelemetry = require("@opentelemetry/sdk-node");
const { getNodeAutoInstrumentations } =
    require(«@opentelemetry/auto-instrumentations-node");

const sdk = new opentelemetry.NodeSDK({
  traceExporter: new opentelemetry.tracing.
```

```
      ConsoleSpanExporter(),
      instrumentations: [getNodeAutoInstrumentations()]
});

sdk.start();
```

Now, we can call our application with the following command:

```
node -r "./tracing.js" index.js
```

After that, open a browser to the project's URL (by default, http://localhost:3000/) and refresh the page a few times. After a few seconds, you should see some events within your terminal that look similar to this:

```
{
    traceId: '7c25880d655f67e5d8e15b83129dc95e',
    parentId: '934dc0ed012f6e37',
    name: <SELECT>,
    id: <af16347a3fbbf923>,
    kind: 2,
    timestamp: 1650124004289597,
    duration: 1616,
    attributes: {
      <db.system': 'mysql',
      <net.peer.name>: <127.0.0.1>,
      <net.peer.port': 3306,
      <db.connection_string':'jdbc:mysql://127.0.0.1:3306/
          airline>,
      <db.name>: <airline>,
      <db.user': 'root',
      <db.statement': 'SELECT `id`, `planeModel`,
          `totalSeats`, `createdAt`, `updatedAt` FROM
          `Airplanes` AS `Airplane`;>
    },
    status: { code: 0 },
    events: []
}
```

Traditionally, the application would export this data to a collector such as Zipkin (https://zipkin.io/), Jaeger (https://www.jaegertracing.io/), or Prometheus (https://prometheus.io/). For instructions on how to associate the application's telemetry data, you can refer to this tutorial here: https://opentelemetry.io/docs/instrumentation/js/exporters/.

If you were to use Zipkin as your collector, then under the const tracerProvider = new NodeTracerProvider({ block within models/index.js, we would replace this line:

```
provider.addSpanProcessor(new BatchSpanProcessor(new
    ZipkinExporter()))
```

We need to replace it with the following:

```
tracerProvider.addSpanProcessor(new BatchSpanProcessor(new
    ZipkinExporter()));
```

This will tell our trace provider to export the traces and logs to the Zipkin Exporter (multiple exporters can be used at the same time).

Summary

In this chapter, we went through the different overload signatures for configuring logging with Sequelize. We also learned how to integrate third-party frameworks, such as OpenTelemetry, within our Node.js application.

In the next chapter, we will be covering how to integrate plugins, or adapters, into our Sequelize instance. The following chapter will also demonstrate how to create our own adapter.

9
Using and Creating Adapters

After developing for several years, you may have a set of common utility functions, a collection of other frameworks, and a library of your own scripts. Maintaining all of these moving parts may become too entropic for an enterprise project or a fleet of microservices. We can restructure our common code into a more generic interface, or pattern, and reclassify those scripts as an "adapter" (also known as a "plugin").

Using adapters can save us development time, prevent us from repeating ourselves, and help centralize collaboration by maintaining its code base. A few examples of an adapter would be transforming text into a specific character ruleset, scaffolding a sidecar project such as an administrative dashboard, or providing a caching layer.

Sequelize offers a way to extend its behavior by allowing the integration of adapters and plugins through a mixture of object prototyping and its lifecycle events. Once we become familiar with using pre-existing adapters, we will create our own adapter/extension for Sequelize that will generate "slug URLs" for each instance within a model.

In this chapter, we will be covering the following topics:

- Installing, configuring, and integrating AdminJS with Sequelize
- Integrating Sequelize with GraphQL
- Creating our own adapter

Technical requirements

You can find the code files of this chapter on GitHub at `https://github.com/PacktPublishing/Supercharging-Node.js-Applications-with-Sequelize/tree/main/ch9`

Installing, configuring, and integrating AdminJS with Sequelize

AdminJS is an administrative dashboard that can integrate into various database management systems, ORMs, and web frameworks. In addition to AdminJS being able to generate charts and tables for your data, it can also create roles and access control lists, export reports, and centralize the modeling of **Create, Read, Update, Delete (CRUD)** operations.

Avalon Airline's investors want us to have a dashboard that allows us to manage flights and tickets, and show basic reporting numbers, such as the total number of planes and gross profit. AdminJS seems to be a perfect fit here; we can begin by installing the necessary components within Avalon Airline's root directory.

Within the terminal, we can install the packages by executing the following command:

```
npm i adminjs @adminjs/express express-formidable @adminjs/
sequelize tslib express-session
```

> **Note**
> The express-formidable module is required as a peer dependency for the @adminjs/
> express package. The formidable module is a fast-streaming multipart parser with a low
> memory footprint. For more information on formidable and its capabilities, you can refer to its
> GitHub repository, located at https://github.com/node-formidable/formidable.

Depending on which version of npm you have installed (eight or above), and which version of @adminjs/sequelize is installed, you may run into legacy peer dependency issues. Due to one of our packages (@adminjs/sequelize) requiring an old module path for Sequelize (sequelize versus @sequelize/core) we will run into missing dependency issues which could be resolved by enabling legacy-peer-deps or using the override option.

Typically, we would want to avoid using the legacy-peer-deps option to avoid breaking changes. We could use the override option in *package.json* for resolving packages which is explained more at https://docs.npmjs.com/cli/v8/configuring-npm/package-json#overrides. Within the *package.json* file, below the scripts block, we will want to add another block with the following:

```
"overrides": {
  "sequelize": "^6"
},
```

If the previous npm installation step failed, we can retry after the *package.json* updates which will resolve @adminjs/sequelize package's sequelize version requirements.

Now, we can start integrating AdminJS into our application. Within the `index.js` file, at the very top, we can add the following lines, which will load the necessary AdminJS modules:

```
const AdminJS = require("adminjs");
const AdminJSExpress = require("@adminjs/express");
const AdminJSSequelize = require("@adminjs/sequelize");
```

Below the `const models = require("./models");` line, we can now add the following line, which will register the Sequelize adapter for AdminJS:

```
AdminJS.registerAdapter(AdminJSSequelize);
```

Below that line, we can add our AdminJS instance and build the Express router:

```
const adminJs = new AdminJS({
    databases: [models.sequelize],
    resources: [
        models.Airplane,
        models.BoardingTicket,
        models.Customer,
        models.FlightSchedule,
        models.Receipts,
    ],
    rootPath: '/admin',
});

const router = AdminJSExpress.buildRouter(adminJs);
```

`model.sequelize` is the instance that we created from `models/index.js`. This will instruct AdminJS to use Sequelize for our connection. The `resources` key holds a list of all of the models that should be exposed/applicable to AdminJS. `rootPath` will be AdminJS' URL prefix for our web application.

Within `index.js`, below the `app.use(bodyParser.json({ type: 'application/json' }));` line, we can now add the AdminJS middleware to help integrate into Express:

```
app.use(adminJs.options.rootPath, router);
```

Now, when we launch our browser to `http://localhost:3000/admin`, we should see a similar page to *Figure 9.1*.

> **Note**
>
> In the next chapter, *Deploying a Sequelize Application*, we will cover how to password-protect your application to prevent an unwanted guest from modifying the database.

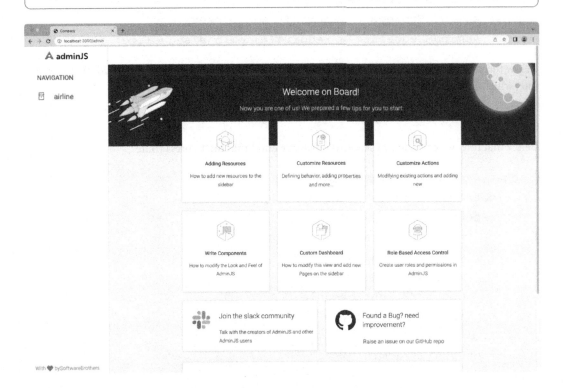

Figure 9.1 – AdminJS welcome dashboard

On the left-side navigation, we should see our database labeled as **airline**. Clicking on that link will reveal our exposed Sequelize models. Clicking on **Airplanes** will show a brief table with our model's data, similar to *Figure 9.2*:

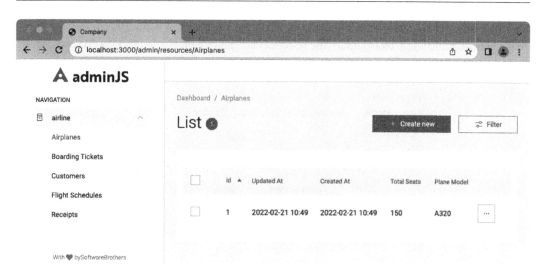

Figure 9.2 – The Airplanes model table

There is a small caveat with AdminJS; at the time of writing, AdminJS does not support Sequelize's virtual data types, which are not text values. Our `BoardingTickets` model contains a virtual type as a Boolean value. When we click on the **Boarding Tickets** menu item, we will be greeted with an error similar to *Figure 9.3*.

Figure 9.3 – AdminJS Displaying an Error From Virtual Types

To fix this issue, we can remove the property's visibility by extending our options for AdminJS' resources. In the new `AdminJS (...)` block, under the resources key, replace the `models.BoardingTicket` line with the following:

```
{
    resource: models.BoardingTicket,
    options: {
        properties: {
            isEmployee: {
                isVisible: false,
            }
        }
    }
},
```

This will instruct AdminJS to disable the `isEmployee` attribute's visibility to `false`. Now, when we refresh the page, the error should no longer be displayed, as shown in *Figure 9.4*.

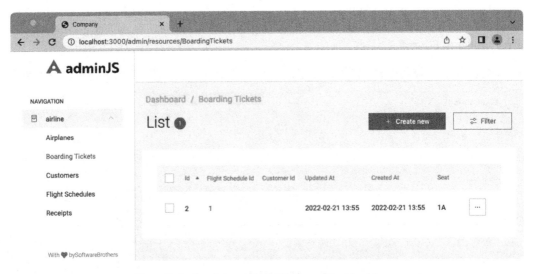

Figure 9.4 – Resolving AdminJS' error with virtual types

> **Note**
>
> For a complete reference on what kind of settings are tunable for AdminJS' property configuration, you can refer to the API documentation here: `https://docs.adminjs.co/PropertyOptions.html`.

AdminJS will also automatically integrate into Sequelize's validation system. So, if we were to edit one of our flight schedules and entered an invalid airport, we would be presented with an error like the one shown in *Figure 9.5*.

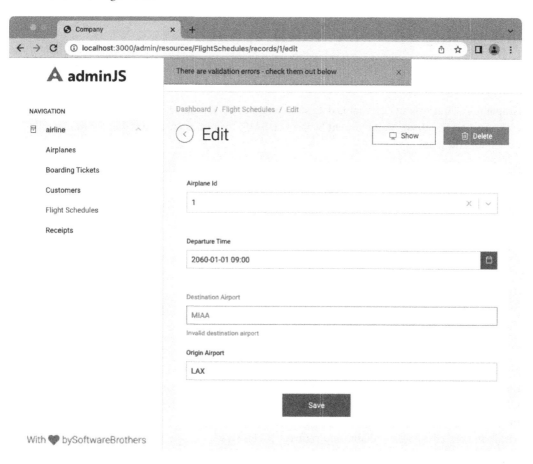

Figure 9.5 – AdminJS validation integration

When we initialized our application with AdminJS, you may have noticed a new folder was automatically created called .adminjs within the project's root directory. The files within this directory are local to your instance only and are neither applicable to deployments nor to other team members.

> **Note**
>
> You may have noticed a .gitignore file that contains .adminjs as part of its content. The .gitignore file is for preventing folders, files, matching paths, and so on from being committed within the git's object space. If you are working within a project using version control, such as Git, then it is recommended to ignore the .adminjs directory from being committed.

Whether adding, deleting, modifying, or validating records, AdminJS offers a very convenient way of managing models. Sometimes, convenience can get in the way, and we would need to view or modify our records in ways that AdminJS cannot. One way to achieve this is to use a GraphQL library.

Integrating Sequelize with GraphQL

GraphQL offers a few advantages over alternatives such as REST. We can declare data shapes with strong types, associate relational hierarchies, and reduce the number of requests required when querying data.

GraphQL is a query language that is data storage-agnostic. You can associate a GraphQL model with a typical **Database Management System (DBMS)**, or just as an abstraction for model validation and shaping.

Here is an example of a GraphQL schema definition:

```
type User {
  name: String!
  bio: String
  roles: [Role!]!
}
type Role {
  name: String!
}
```

The `User` type has three attributes, with the `name` and `roles` being required (indicated with the exclamation mark), while the `bio` definition is an optional string. Within this example, the `User` type's roles attributes will always return an array with zero or more items from the exclamation mark that sits outside of the brackets ([...] !), and the other exclamation mark indicates that each item within the set will be non-nullable and return a `Role` type.

A type just references an object, but there are two types that are reserved for GraphQL itself, the `Query` and the `Mutation` type. The query types are reserved for defining input parameters and relations, and associations, of a collection of types. `Mutation` types are utilized when we want to modify our data. You can think of queries as GET requests and mutation queries as a combination of POST and PUT HTTP methods.

To query the previous example's types, we will invoke a query type like so:

```
type Query {
  query usersByName ($name: String!) {
    users (name: $name) {
      name
```

```
      bio
      roles {
        name
      }
    }
  }
}
```

This example will generate a function called `usersByName` with an input parameter of a required string. The function would yield any `User` types whose name matches the `$name` variable. Each record would return the name, bio, and an array of roles associated with that user. The data shape that is returned would look similar to the following:

```
{
    "data": {
        "usersByName": {
            "users": [
                {
                    "name": "Bob",
                    "bio": "Programmer",
                    "roles": []
                },
                {
                    "name": "Bob",
                    "bio": "Lead",
                    "roles": [{"name": "Admin"}]
                }
            ]
        }
    }
}
```

Mick Hansen, one of the original maintainers of Sequelize, created an NPM package called sequelize-graphql that will help bridge our models with a GraphQL type definition. To get started on using GraphQL with Sequelize in our current project, we will need to install the following NPM modules:

```
npm i --save graphql-sequelize @graphql-yoga/node graphql-relay
```

The graphql-sequelize library may require old, or conflicting, versions for the graphql and graphql-relay library. We would need to modify our override object within the *package.json* file to the following to resolve those issues:

```
"overrides": {
  "graphql": "^15",
  "graphql-relay": "^0.10.0",
  "sequelize": "^6"
},
```

The graphql-yoga package is a GraphQL server framework dedicated to performance and ease of use. Its GitHub repository can be found here: https://github.com/dotansimha/graphql-yoga.

The first step is to add a static constant called tableName for each model, with the value being the model's table name for the sequelize-graphql plugin.

We will start with the models/airplane.js file; under the class Airplane extends Model line, add the following variable:

```
static tableName = 'Airplanes';
```

Within models/boardingticket.js, under the class BoardingTicket extends Model line, add the following variable:

```
static tableName = 'BoardingTickets';
```

Within models/customer.js, under the class Customer extends Model line, add the following variable:

```
static tableName = 'Customers';
```

Within models/flightschedule.js, under the class FlightSchedule extends Model line, add the following variable:

```
static tableName = 'FlightSchedules';
```

Within models/receipts.js, under the class Receipts extends Model line, add the following variable:

```
static tableName = 'Receipts';
```

Now, we can begin with declaring our type definitions and query resolver patterns for the GraphQL server. Within the project's root directory, add a new file called `graphql.js`, starting with the following `require` commands:

```
const { createServer } = require("@graphql-yoga/node");
const { resolver } = require("graphql-sequelize");
const models = require("./models");
```

Next, we want to start defining our query interface for when we want to execute queries later. You may think of this as something similar to a header file in a "C" language project:

```
const typeDefs = `
  type Query {
    airplane(id: ID!): Airplane
    airplanes: [Airplane]

    boardingTicket(id: ID!): BoardingTicket
    boardingTickets: [BoardingTicket]

    customer(id: ID!): Customer
    customers: [Customer]

    flightSchedule(id: ID!): FlightSchedule
    flightSchedules: [FlightSchedule]

    receipt(id: ID!): Receipt
    receipts: [Receipt]
  }
```

While keeping the `typeDef` variable open, we can add a simple `Mutation` query example:

```
  type Mutation {
    upsertAirplane(name: String!, data: AirplaneInput!):
    Airplane
  }

  input AirplaneInput {
    planeModel: String
    totalSeats: Int
  }
```

```
type Airplane {
  id: ID!
  planeModel: String
  totalSeats: Int

  schedules: [FlightSchedule]
}
```

Next, we can add our model schematics to the definitions:

```
type Airplane {
  id: ID!
  planeModel: String
  totalSeats: Int

  schedules: [FlightSchedule]
}

type BoardingTicket {
  id: ID!
  seat: String

  owner: Customer
}

type Customer {
  id: ID!
  name: String
  email: String

  tickets: [BoardingTicket]
}

type FlightSchedule {
  id: ID!
  originAirport: String
  destinationAirport: String
  departureTime: String
}
```

```
    type Receipt {
      id: ID!
      receipt: String
    }
`;
```

Next, we will want to set our resolvers to associate the type definitions with the correct Sequelize model associations. Let's start with the query resolvers:

```
const resolvers = {
  Query: {
    airplane: resolver(models.Airplane),
    airplanes: resolver(models.Airplane),
    boardingTicket: resolver(models.BoardingTicket),
    boardingTickets: resolver(models.BoardingTicket),
    customer: resolver(models.Customer),
    customers: resolver(models.Customer),
    flightSchedule: resolver(models.FlightSchedule),
    flightSchedules: resolver(models.FlightSchedule),
    receipt: resolver(models.Receipts),
    receipts: resolver(models.Receipts),
  },
```

Next, we can add a `Mutation` resolver example:

```
  Mutation: {
    async upsertAirplane(parent, args, ctx, info) {
        const [airplane, created] = await models.Airplane.
        findOrCreate({
            where: {
                planeModel: args.name
            },
            defaults: (args.data || {}),
        });

        // if we created the record we do not need to
           update it
        if (created) {
            return airplane;
        }
```

```
        if (typeof args.data !== "undefined") {
            await airplane.update(args.data);
        }

        return airplane;
    }
  },
```

Then, we can resolve our model associations and close the variable:

```
  Airplane: {
    schedules: resolver(models.Airplane.FlightSchedules),
  },
  BoardingTicket: {
    owner: resolver(models.BoardingTicket.Customer),
  },
  Customer: {
    tickets: resolver(models.Customer.BoardingTickets),
  },
};
```

Finally, we can create our server with the schema definitions and export it:

```
const server = new createServer({
  schema: {
    typeDefs,
    resolvers,
  }
});

module.exports = { server };
```

Within the `index.js` file, in the project's root directory, we can add the following line under our `var models = require("./models")` line:

```
const { server } = require("./graphql");
```

After we have mounted the AdminJS router, `app.use(adminJs.options.rootPath, router)`, add the following line:

```
app.use('/graphql', server);
```

After we have finished our `index.js` modifications, we can start our application:

```
npm run start
```

Once the server is up and running, we can access GraphQL Yoga's dashboard interface (*Figure 9.6*) by visiting the following URL within a browser: `http://localhost:3000/graphql`:

> **Note**
>
> In a production deployment, we would either want to disable this route based on the value of `process.env.NODE_ENV` or add authentication-based middleware to the `/graphql` route in `index.js`.

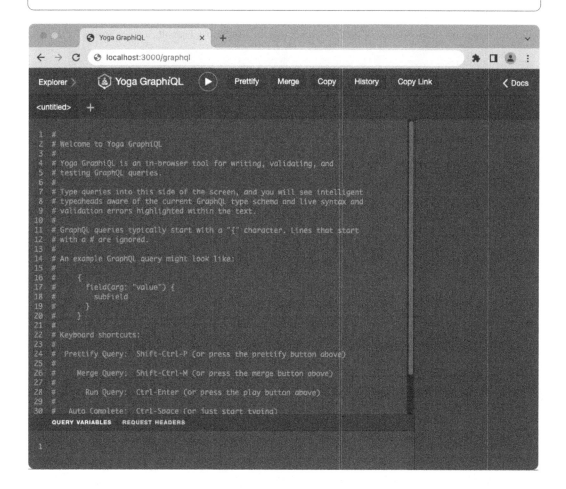

Figure 9.6 – The GraphQL Yoga dashboard

We can test our queries and resolvers by executing queries within this dashboard. Remove all of the current content on the notepad section of the dashboard and enter the following:

```
{
  airplanes {
    id
    planeModel
    totalSeats
  }
}
```

There should be a "play button" at the top that will execute your query (alternatively, hitting the *Ctrl* and *Enter* keys simultaneously will do the same), which should yield results similar to the following:

```
{
  "data": {
    "airplanes": [
      {
        "id": "1",
        "planeModel": "A320",
        "totalSeats": 150
      }
    ]
  }
}
```

If we wanted to update our airplane's model name, we could use a `mutation` query:

```
mutation {
  upsertAirplane(name:"A320", data:{planeModel:"A321"}) {
    planeModel
  }
}
```

This will return the following result:

```
{
  "data": {
    "upsertAirplane": {
      "planeModel": "A321"
```

```
      }
    }
  }
}
```

Within the GraphQL Yoga dashboard, there should be a < **Docs** link at the top right (refer to *Figure 9.6*), which will open a drawer panel. There will then be a **Query** link, which will expose our queries and type definitions. This should help make queries easier within the dashboard.

Now that we have established a connection between a GraphQL server and our Sequelize models and integrated another adapter that provides an easy-to-use admin dashboard, it is time for us to build our own adapter for Sequelize.

Creating our own adapter

Sequelize is fairly extensible through its class properties, lifecycle events, and configurations. For the example of creating our own adapter for Sequelize, we will integrate a new data type that will automatically convert values, using a specific set of rules, to what is called a "slug URL." A slug URL usually consists of hyphens instead of spaces, lowercase lettering, and removes all special characters.

Let's look at the steps to create our adapter:

1. We'll begin by installing any necessary packages. Keeping a copy of a character map of special characters can be a daunting task, so we will use an npm package called, `github-slugger` to help us:

    ```
    npm i --save github-slugger
    ```

2. Next, we will want to create a couple of directories and a file with `plugins/slug/index.js` as the path from the project's root directory. Before we can begin coding within that file, we will need to add the `slug` column to a table within the database. We will use the Airplane model for this example; using the `sequelize-cli` command, we can create a new migration event:

    ```
    sequelize-cli migration:create --name add_slug_to_
    airplanes
    ```

    This command should generate a new file within the `migrations` directory ending in `add_slug_to_airplanes.js`.

3. Replace the file's contents with the following:

    ```
    'use strict';

    module.exports = {
      up: async (queryInterface, Sequelize) => {
    ```

```
      await queryInterface.addColumn(
        'Airplanes',
        'slug',
        {
          type: Sequelize.STRING,
          allowNull: true,
        },
      );

      await queryInterface.addIndex(
        'Airplanes',
        ['slug'],
        {
          name: 'airplanes_slug_uniq_idx',
          unique: true,
        },
      );
    },

  down: async (queryInterface, Sequelize) => {
    await queryInterface.removeIndex('Airplanes',
    'airplanes_slug_uniq_idx');
    await queryInterface.removeColumn('Airplanes',
    'slug');
    },
};
```

This will instruct Sequelize to create a new column in the `Airplanes` table called `slug` as a text value, along with a unique index that is associated with that column.

4. To perform the latest migration, we will run the `db:migrate` command:

    sequelize-cli db:migrate

After the column has been added to the Airplanes table, we will need to add the attribute manually to the `models/airplanes.js` file.

5. Replace the `totalSeats` attribute block with the following:

```
totalSeats: {
  type: DataTypes.INTEGER,
  validate: {
    min: {
      args: 1,
      msg: 'A plane must have at least one seat'
    }
  }
},
slug: {
  type: DataTypes.STRING,
  unique: true,
},
```

6. In the `graphql.js` file, we will want to add the `slug` column to the `Airplane` type definition as well:

```
type Airplane {
  id: ID!
  planeModel: String
  totalSeats: Int
  slug: String

  schedules: [FlightSchedule]
}
```

7. Now, we can begin editing the `plugins/slug/index.js` file, starting with the following lines of code:

```
const slug = require("github-slugger").slug;

class SlugPlugin {
    use(model, options) {
        const DEFAULTS = {
            column: 'slug',
            source: 'name',
            transaction: null,
```

```
};

options = {...DEFAULTS, ...options};
```

This will create a `SlugPlugin` class with one method called `use`. The input parameters are the `model` class, a couple of options, and their defaults.

8. Underneath those blocks, we will create our `generateSlug` method:

```
// concat the fields for the slug
function generateSlug(instance, fields) {
    return slug(fields.map((field) =>
    instance[field]));
}
```

9. Next, we will want to ensure that a slug does not exist prior to updating. We will want to create some sort of finder method and an increment method for funding a unique value. We can start with the finder method shown here:

```
async function findSlug(slug) {
    return await model.findOne({
        where: {
            [options.column]: slug
        },
        transaction: options.transaction ||
        null,
    });
}
```

10. Now for the incremental method; this function will run in a loop until a unique match is found using a combination of the slug's value and an integer. Ideally, in a real production environment, we would come up with a cleverer way of finding unique values (for example, appending a hash instead of an incremental variable), but for brevity, we will create this function:

```
async function incrementSuffix(slugVal) {
    let found = false;
    let cnt = 1;
    let suffix = "";

    while (!found) {
        suffix = `${slugVal}-${cnt}`;
```

```
            found = await findSlug(suffix);
            cnt++;
        }


        return suffix;
    }
```

11. We can now begin creating the main event function. First, we will check whether our slug's applicable attributes (the `planeModel` attribute, in this example) have been modified. If they have not been changed, then we will skip the entire event, since there is nothing to be done:

```
async function onSaveOrUpdate(instance) {
    const changed = options.source.
    some(function (field) {
        return instance.changed(field);
    });

    if (!changed) {
        return instance;
    }
```

12. Next, we will compare the current value with the newly generated value. If they are the same (for example, a letter casing change), then simply skip the event:

```
    let curVal = instance[options.column];
    let newVal = generateSlug(instance,
    options.source);

    if (curVal !== null && curVal == newVal) {
        return instance;
    }
```

13. Now, we can check and see whether the newly generated value is unique and, if so, set the instance's `slug` attribute to that value and return the instance:

```
    let slugExist = await findSlug(newVal);

    if (!slugExist) {
        instance[options.column] = newVal;
        return instance;
    }
```

14. Otherwise, we will want to use our `incrementSuffix` method and return the instance afterward:

```
newVal = await incrementSuffix(newVal);
instance[options.column] = newVal;


return instance;
```

15. Afterward, we can close our `event` method, attach the method to the model's lifecycle events, and close the `SlugPlugin` class:

```
    }


    // use the lifecycle events for invoking the
      onSaveOrUpdate event
    model.addHook('beforeCreate', onSaveOrUpdate);
    model.addHook('beforeUpdate', onSaveOrUpdate);

  }

}
```

16. Finally, we can export an instance of our plugin as well as the class definition itself:

```
const instance = new SlugPlugin();

module.exports = instance;
module.exports.SlugPlugin = instance;
```

17. Within the `models/airplanes.js` file, we will want to integrate our new plugin with the model. At the top of the file, we can include the plugin like so:

```
const slugPlugin = require('../plugins/slug');
```

18. After the model's definition, and before the `return Airplane` line, we can associate the `slug` plugin with the model:

```
slugPlugin.use(Airplane, {
  source: ['planeModel']
});
```

This will tell our plugin to use the `planeModel` attribute as the source field when generating the slug's value.

19. In order to test our plugin, we can go to our GraphQL dashboard located at `http://localhost:3000/graphql` and enter the following command:

```
mutation {
  upsertAirplane(name:"A321", data:{planeModel:
  "A321 B"}) {
    planeModel
    totalSeats
    slug
  }
}
```

This will find, and update, our A321 airplane's `planeModel` value along with setting a `slug` value, as shown here:

```
{
  "data": {
    "upsertAirplane": {
      "planeModel": "A321 B",
      "totalSeats": 150,
      "slug": "a321-b"
    }
  }
}
```

This finalizes our custom Sequelize adapter section. You can use the `plugins/slug/index.js` adapter in any other project using Sequelize. Feel free to add `slug` columns to other models, but make sure to follow the necessary steps:

1. Generate a migration file and migrate the column changes to the database.

2. Update the `graphql.js` file with the appropriate type definitions.

3. Include the `plugin` library within the applicable models' files and associate the plugin with the models using the `use` method.

Summary

In this chapter, we went through the process of installing a dashboard that integrates with a database, integrating GraphQL using a third-party library, and creating our own Sequelize adapter that will automatically add slug values.

In the next chapter, we will start developing our website to be more production-ready and feature-complete. Some of these features include listing schedules, ordering tickets, and entering customer information.

10

Deploying a Sequelize Application

After installing an admin dashboard, configuring our web application to book flights, and having built a backend server, we are now ready to start developing the frontend interface along with deploying the application. Just in time too, because our board members want to see some progress, and they would like to see a working prototype for purchasing a ticket.

Throughout this chapter, and to meet the requirements of our board members, we will need to do the following:

- Refactor some of our current routes and add another route for listing flight schedules
- Integrate Express' static middleware and secure the admin interface
- Create a page to list and book flights
- Deploy the application to a service such as Fly.io

Technical requirements

For the tasks in this chapter, we will be installing the following additional software:

- A version control manager called Git
- The Fly.io CLI for deploying to a cloud application platform

You can find the code files for this chapter on GitHub at `https://github.com/PacktPublishing/Supercharging-Node.js-Applications-with-Sequelize/tree/main/ch10`.

Refactoring and adding flight schedule routes

Before we start creating the customer interface for purchasing a boarding ticket, we will need to make several adjustments to our code base. Let us begin by creating a new file located at `routes/ airplanes.js` and moving the `app.post('/airplanes', …)` and `app.get('/ airplanes/:id', …)` blocks into that file as follows:

```
async function getAirplane(req, res) {
    const airplane = await models.Airplane.findByPk
     (req.params.id);
    if (!airplane) {
        return res.sendStatus(404);
    }

    res.json(airplane);
}
exports.getAirplane = getAirplane;
```

This route will return an `Airplane` model record based on the primary key, which is defined in Express' Request object (indicated by the `:id` symbol). If there were no records to be found, then we will return a `404` (not found) status.

Next, we will take the `createAirplane` code block from `routes/flights.js` and move it into the `routes/airplanes.js` file:

```
async function createAirplane(req, res) {
    const { name, seats } = req.body;

    try {
        const airplane = await models.Airplane.create({
            planeModel: name,
            totalSeats: seats,
        });

        return res.json(airplane);
    } catch (error) {
        res.status(500).send(error);
    }
}
exports.createAirplane = createAirplane;
```

Within `routes/flights.js`, we will want to add a new handler called `flightSchedules`:

```
async function flightSchedules(req, res) {
    const records = await models.FlightSchedule.findAll({
        include: [models.Airplane]
    });


    res.json(records);
}
exports.flightSchedules = flightSchedules;
```

After that, within the `index.js` file, in the project's root directory, we can remove the `app.get('/', …)` block and modify the route requiring blocks (just above the block that we removed) to match the new method paths as follows:

```
const { bookTicket } = require("./routes/tickets")
const { createSchedule, flightSchedules } =
require("./routes/flights");
const { getAirplane, createAirplane } =
require("./routes/airplanes");
```

The `app.get('/airplanes/:id', …)` block should now look as follows:

```
app.get('/airplanes/:id', getAirplane);
```

And below that, we can add the flight schedule route:

```
app.get('/flights', flightSchedules);
```

Next, we will want to adjust the error returned from the customers model. Within `models/customers.js`, replace the existing attributes with the following code:

```
    name: {
      type: DataTypes.STRING,
      validate: {
        notEmpty: {
            msg: "A name is required for the customer",
        }
      }
    },
    email: {
```

```
      type: DataTypes.STRING,
      validate: {
        isEmail: {
            msg: "Invalid email format for the customer",
        }
      }
    }
```

The last modification for flights and booking a ticket involves making some adjustments to the routes/tickets.js file. First, we will want to add Sequelize's ValidationError at the top of the file:

```
const { ValidationError } = require("@sequelize/core");
```

Since we will be finding, or creating, a customer throughout the booking process, we will want to change the req.body line to this:

```
const { scheduleId, seat, name, email } = req.body;
```

And below that line, we will add the following:

```
const [customer] = await models.Customer.findOrCreate({
    where: {
        email,
    },
    defaults: {
        name,
    }
});
```

This will tell Sequelize to find or create a customer record using the email as a key and will hydrate the record with the name (if the record is new) from the POST request.

Just above the await schedule.addBoardingTicket(...) block, we will want to add a method that defines the customer association for the newly created boarding ticket:

```
await boardingTicket.setCustomer(
  customer,
  { transaction: tx }
);
```

The remaining modification for this file is replacing the `catch` block with the following code:

```
} catch (error) {
    if (error instanceof ValidationError) {
        let errObj = {};

        error.errors.map(err => {
            errObj[err.path] = err.message;
        });

        return res.status(400).json(errObj);
    }

    if (error instanceof Error) {
        return res.status(400).send(error.message);
    }

    return res.status(400).send(error.toString());
}
```

This error block will check whether the incoming error is a Sequelize `ValidationError` type and if so, will map out the errors to `errorObj` with the column (`err.path`) as a key and the error message (`err.message`) as the value – then, it will return the `error` object. The next `if` block will check whether the error is a generic `Error` type, and if so, return the `error.message` value – otherwise, it will return the `error` variable as a string. This will provide a more ergonomic way of handling errors for a quick prototype website.

Those are all of the modifications that are necessary for managing flights and creating flight tickets. The next step is to set the foundation for our static assets and secure our admin dashboard.

Integrating Express' static middleware and securing the admin interface

Before exposing our application to the general public, we will need to secure the admin dashboard routes, along with exposing the static assets for frontend development. First, we will want to create a new directory with an empty file located at `public/index.html`. After that, we can start making modifications to the `index.js` file (within the project's root directory). At the top, we will need Node.js' path module:

```
const path = require("path");
```

Just below the `app.use('/graphql', server)` block, we will want to tell Express to serve static assets that are found within the public directory:

```
app.use(express.static(path.join(__dirname, "public")));
```

Express will try to find a matching file with the associated route in the public directory before cascading down to our API routes (for example, `/airplanes` or `/flights`). The reason why we use `path.join` here is to avoid mismatches from relative paths, which allows us to run the application from any directory.

Next, we will want to secure our admin dashboard – in the name of brevity, we will use the HTTP authentication method. This will require us to install the `express-basic-auth` package:

```
npm i --save express-basic-auth
```

Add the requirement at the top of `index.js`:

```
const basicAuth = require("express-basic-auth");
```

Replace the `app.use(adminJs.options.rootPath, router)` block with the following:

```
app.use(adminJs.options.rootPath, basicAuth({
        users: { 'admin': 'supersecret' }, challenge: true,
        }), router);
```

This will tell Express to ask for a username and password combination (admin and `supersecret` respectively) when accessing the AdminJS root path. Now, when we start our application and head over to `http://localhost:3000/admin`, we should be greeted by a login dialog similar to that in *Figure 10.1*:

Figure 10.1 – Admin login

Now that our AdminJS routes are secure, we can start creating the frontend page that our customers will see when they visit the application.

> **Note**
>
> In a real-world scenario application, instead of using basic authentication, we would use another form of authentication such as JSON Web Tokens or a Single Sign-On Service.

Creating a page to list and book flights

For this application, we will be requiring two external libraries to help build the frontend components for the application. The first library is **Bulma**, which is a CSS framework designed for quick prototyping and doesn't require its own JavaScript library. For more information on Bulma, you can visit its website, located at `https://bulma.io/`. The next library is **AlpineJS**, which is a framework that helps us avoid writing JavaScript to modify states or behaviors by using HTML tags and markup. More information can be found at `https://alpinejs.dev/`.

> **Note**
>
> Other fantastic frontend frameworks that can be used instead of AlpineJS include VueJS, React, or Deepkit. AlpineJS was chosen for this book due to its minimal setup and requirements.

Let us start with the bare necessities, the HTML for a simple header section of the website:

1. Within `public/index.html`, add the following code:

    ```html
    <!DOCTYPE html>
    <html>

    <head>
      <meta charset="utf-8">
      <meta name="viewport" content="width=device-width,
    initial-scale=1">
      <title>Welcome to Avalon Airlines!</title>
      <link rel="stylesheet" href="https://cdn.jsdelivr.net/
    npm/bulma@0.9.4/css/bulma.min.css">
      <script src="https://unpkg.com/alpinejs@3.10.3/dist/
    cdn.min.js" defer></script>
    </head>

    <body>
    ```

```
<section class="section">
  <div class="container">
    <h1 class="title">
      Welcome to Avalon Airlines!
    </h1>
    <p class="subtitle">
      Where would you like to go
      <strong>today</strong>?
    </p>
  </div>
</section>

</body>

</html>
```

2. After the first `<section>`, we will want to add another with a container separated by two columns as follows:

```
<section class="section">
  <div class="container">
    <div class="columns" x-data="{
              flights: [],
              selected: {}
            }" x-init="fetch('/flights')
                .then(res => res.json())
                .then(res => flights = res)">
      <div class="column">
      </div>

      <div class="column">
      </div>
    </div>
  </div>
</section>
```

The `x-data` attribute will tell AlpineJS what kind of shape our model and data will hold. This data will be propagated down to children elements. The `x-init` attribute will run upon initialization of the element and will fetch from our API calling `/flights`. Afterward, we take the results and convert them into a JSON object and then we assign the JSON response to the `flights` array within our `x-data` attribute.

3. In the first column, from the section that we just created, we will want to create a table that renders all of the available flights:

```
<table class="table is-bordered is-striped is-narrow
is-hoverable is-fullwidth">
    <thead>
      <tr>
        <th>Origin</th>
        <th>Departure</th>
        <th>Departure Time</th>
        <th>Model</th>
        <th></th>
      </tr>
    </thead>
    <tbody>
      <template x-for="flight in flights">
        <tr>
          <td x-text="flight.originAirport"></td>
          <td x-text="flight.destinationAirport"></td>
          <td x-text="flight.departureTime"></td>
          <td x-text=
            "flight.Airplane.planeModel"></td>
          <td><button x-on:click="selected = flight"
            class="button is-primary is-light is-
            small">Book
                Flight</button></td>
        </tr>
      </template>
    </tbody>
  </table>
```

AlpineJS will recognize the x-for attribute, which operates similarly to for loops in other languages – anything inside of that block will be rendered for each iteration. If the flights array is empty, then the template block will not be rendered. The x-on:click attribute will add a click event listener to the button element, which will assign the selected variable (part of our x-data model from the parent element) to the associated flight entry.

4. Next, we will want to create the logic for handling our form submission. Just above the closing body tag (</body>), we will want to add the following:

```
<script>
  function flightForm() {
    return {
      data: {
        email: "",
        name: "",
        seat: "",
        success: false,
      },
      formMessages: [],
      loading: false,
```

The data, formMessages, and loading variables are all states for AlpineJS. We can choose whatever names we want, as it does not matter for AlpineJS.

5. Now, for the submission event handling part, just below the loading: false block, add the following:

```
submit(e) {
  this.loading = true;

  fetch("/book-flight", {
    method: "POST",
    headers: {
      "Content-Type": "application/json",
      "Accept": "application/json",
    },
    body: JSON.stringify({
      ...this.data,
      scheduleId: this.selected.id,
```

```
    }),
  })
```

Once the submit event has been invoked, a `POST /book-flight` request is made with the necessary JSON headers and body parameters. The `this.selected.id` variable will reference our parent's element's `x-data` model.

6. After the fetch, we will need to handle the appropriate responses. Let us start with a successful path and add the following code just after the fetch block:

```
.then(async (response) => {
  const { headers, ok, message, body } =
    response;

  const isJson = headers.get('content-
    type')?.includes('application/json');
  const data = isJson ? await
    response.json() : await response.text();

  if (!ok) {
    return Promise.reject(isJson ?
      Object.values(data) : data);
  }

  // boarding ticket was successfully created
  this.formMessages = [];
  this.data = {
    email: "",
    name: "",
    seat: this.data.seat,
    success: true,
  }
})
```

This method will check whether the data is JSON or plain text. Then, it will check whether the response is OK (and return a rejected promise if it returned errors). If the ticket was successfully created, we will reset the email, name, and seat to their initial values and set `success` to `true`.

> **Note**
>
> We are setting the name and email to empty strings in the previous example to clear out the current form's data. If we were to omit these explicit values, then AlpineJS would show the name and email inputs with their previous values when the `flightForm` appears on the screen.

7. After that, we can add the `catch` and `finally` blocks and close the remaining script:

```
            .catch((err) => {
                this.formMessages = Array.isArray(err) ?
                    err : [err];
            })
            .finally(() => {
                this.loading = false;
            });
        },
    };
}
</script>
```

The caught error will propagate itself to `formMessages` as an array and regardless of success or failure, we will want to use the `finally` block to set the loading state to `false`.

8. Let's return to the section with the two columns that we created earlier – in the second column, we will want to add a success message as well as the form itself. We will start with a section that displays information about the currently selected flight for our form:

```
<div x-show="!!selected.id">
  <section class="hero is-info">
    <div class="hero-body">
      <p class="title">
        <span x-text="selected.originAirport"></span>
&#8594; <span x-text="selected.destinationAirport">
        </span>
      </p>
      <p class="subtitle">
        Departs at <span x-text="selected.
        departureTime"></span>
      </p>
    </div>
  </section>
```

The x-show attribute will hide an element if the value yields as true. The next few elements will use the data from our selected object property from the parent element's x-data model. This element should be hidden until we select a flight. The x-text attribute will tell AlpineJS to render the element's innerText to the value associated with the attribute (for example, selected.originAirport, or selected.departureTime).

9. Once the hero section is setup, we will add a form for the success message when a flight is successfully booked:

```html
<form x-data="flightForm()" @submit.prevent="submit">
  <div x-show="!!data.success">
    <section class="hero is-primary">
      <div class="hero-body">
        <p class="title">
          Your boarding ticket has been created!
        </p>
        <p class="subtitle">
          Your seat for this flight is <span
            x-text="data.seat"></span>
        </p>
      </div>
    </section>
    <div class="mt-4 field is-grouped is-grouped-
      centered">
      <p class="control">
        <a class="button is-light"
          x-on:click="selected = {}; data.success =
          false; data.seat = ''">
          OK
        </a>
      </p>
    </div>
  </div>
```

We encapsulated the states of flightForm and the events within the <form> tag. The @submit.prevent="submit" attribute will tell AlpineJS to prevent bubble propagation when submitting the event and to use our submit function inside of the flightForm method.

Next, we will check to see whether `success` is `true` and if so, show the order confirmation section. We will want some way to reset the state once a client has purchased a ticket (in case they want to purchase another ticket), which is what the `x-on:click` event does when we click the **OK** button.

10. Now, for the actual form, we will check to see whether `data.success` is `false` and if so, show the form with some basic fields. Inside the same `form` attribute, add the following:

```
<div x-show="!data.success">
  <div class="field pt-4">
    <label class="label">Full Name</label>
    <div class="control">
      <input class="input" type="text" x-model=
      "data.name" placeholder="e.g Alex Smith">
    </div>
  </div>

  <div class="field">
    <label class="label">Your Email</label>
    <div class="control">
      <input class="input" type="email"
        x-model="data.email"
        placeholder="e.g. alexsmith@avalon-
        airlines.com">
    </div>
  </div>

  <div class="field">
    <label class="label">Seat Selection</label>
    <div class="control">
      <input class="input" type="text"
        x-model="data.seat" placeholder="e.g. 1A">
    </div>
  </div>
```

The `x-model` attribute will bind the input's value with the `x-data` object (for example, `x-model="data.email"` will associate itself with the `data.email` attribute of `flightForm`).

11. Just below this code, we can add the call-to-action buttons for purchasing a ticket or canceling the order:

```
<div class="field is-grouped is-grouped-centered">
  <p class="control">
    <button type="submit" :disabled="loading"
    class="button is-primary">
      Purchase Ticket
    </button>
  </p>
  <p class="control">
    <a class="button is-light" x-on:click="selected = {};
    data.success = false; formMessages = []">
      Cancel
    </a>
  </p>
</div>
```

The `:disabled` attribute is an AlpineJS shorthand code for disabling a particular element under a specific condition (in our case, this would be the loading variable). Clicking on the **Cancel** button will reset the selected data, set the `data.success` variable to `false`, and make `formMessages` into an empty array.

12. Finally, we can add a template for handling our `formMessages` variable and close the remaining HTML tags:

```
<template x-for="message in
  formMessages">
  <article class="message is-warning">
    <div class="message-header">
      <p>A correction is required</p>
    </div>
    <div x-text="message" class=
      "message-body"></div>
  </article>
</template>
</div>
</form>
```

Our frontend application should now be complete. If we visit `http://localhost:3000/`, it
should look similar to *Figure 10.2*. Clicking on the **Book Flight** button should generate something
similar to *Figure 10.3*:

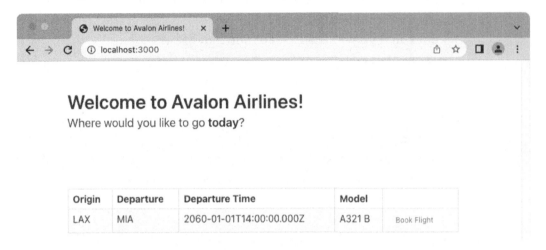

Figure 10.2 – Welcome to Avalon Airlines!

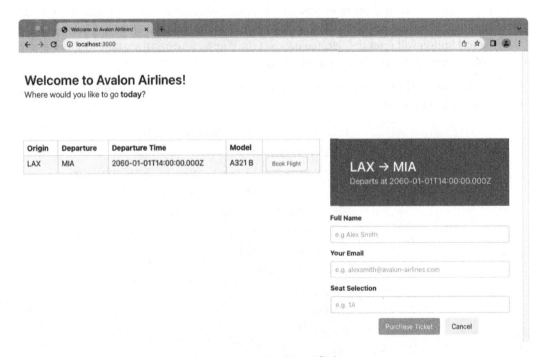

Figure 10.3 – Booking a flight

When we click on **Purchase Ticket** without entering any information, we should be greeted with a few warnings, as shown in *Figure 10.4*:

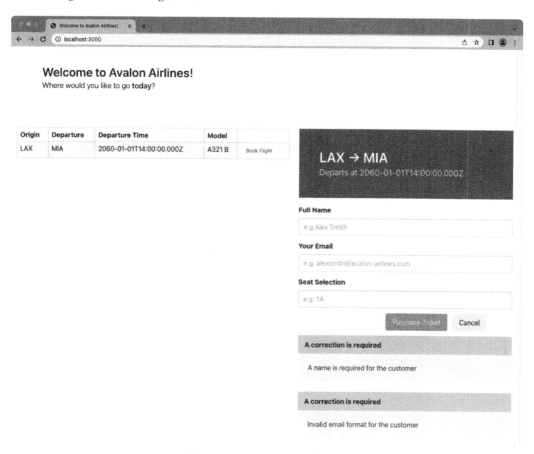

Figure 10.4 – Warnings from Sequelize

When we enter in the appropriate information, the application will create a new customer and boarding ticket along with a success message, as shown in *Figure 10.5*:

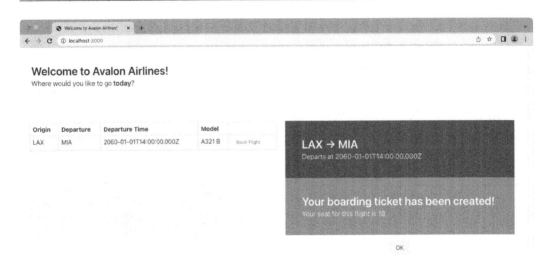

Figure 10.5 – The success message

Visiting the admin dashboard will confirm that our ticket and customer account were created successfully. We can see the boarding tickets at `http://localhost:3000/admin/resources/BoardingTickets` (remember to log in with appropriate credentials), similar to *Figure 10.6*:

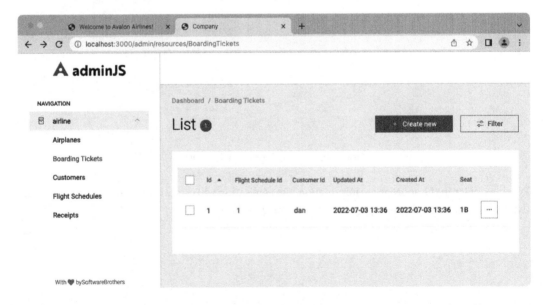

Figure 10.6 – The admin dashboard showing the boarding tickets

It looks as though our application is ready to be deployed. In the next section, we will go over the requirements for setting up an environment on a cloud application platform such as Fly.io.

Deploying the application

Before we begin, we will want to make sure our project is initialized as a git repository, if your machine does not have git installed you may find instruction on how to install the binary here `https://git-scm.com/book/en/v2/Getting-Started-Installing-Git`. If you've been following along, and haven't yet initialized your project as a git repository, you can do so by running the following command in your project's root directory:

```
git init
```

For the deployment process, we will use a cloud hosting service called **Fly.io** (`https://fly.io/`). Fly.io offers a useful command line tool to help us register and authenticate into an account in addition to making application deployments easier. Detailed instructions on getting started with Fly.io's CLI can be found at `https://fly.io/docs/hands-on/install-flyctl/`.

For MacOS users, with Homebrew, we can install the binary with this command:

```
brew install flyctl
```

Linux users can install the binary with this command:

```
curl -L https://fly.io/install.sh | sh
```

For Window users, Fly.io recommends using the PowerShell for downloading the binary:

```
iwr https://fly.io/install.ps1 -useb | iex
```

Once the binary installation has been completed, we will need to login, or register a new account, and then create a new application. If you have not created your free Fly.io account previously, we can use the following command to get started

```
flyctl auth signup
```

Alternatively, we can authenticate ourselves if we had registered an account previously:

```
flyctl auth login
```

After we have authenticated, we can now deploy our application:

```
flyctl launch
```

This command will ask us for an application name and region which we can leave these values as blank or its default value. We will also be asked if we want to create a Postgres database and deploy the application right away which we should decline by entering in the "n" key as a response. The following should look similar to your screen:

```
Creating app in /Users/daniel/Documents/Book/code/ch10
Scanning source code
Detected a NodeJS app
Using the following build configuration:
    Builder: heroku/buildpacks:20
? App Name (leave blank to use an auto-generated name):
Automatically selected personal organization: Daniel Durante
? Select region: iad (Ashburn, Virginia (US))
Created app nameless-shape-3908 in organization personal
Wrote config file fly.toml
? Would you like to set up a Postgresql database now? No
? Would you like to deploy now? No
Your app is ready. Deploy with `flyctl deploy`
```

Don't deploy the application just yet. We will need to enable MySQL with our Fly.io application first. At the moment, Fly.io does not offer a way to sidecar a MySQL database within the same application as our web application. The solution for this is to create a separate a Fly.io application with MySQL only.

In the project's root directory, we will want to create a new folder called, "fly-mysql" and run the following command within that folder:

```
fly launch
```

Respond to the questions the same way we originally did in the previous `fly launch` command. Now, our database will need to be stored somewhere, so let us begin by creating a volume on Fly.io and choosing the same region as the previous step. Within the *fly-mysql* directory run the following command to create a new volume:

```
fly volumes create mysqldata --size 1
```

> **Note**
>
> The "--size" parameter for `fly volumes create <name>` references the number of gigabytes as its unit. For more information about the `volumes` Fly.io subcommand more information can be found at `https://fly.io/docs/reference/volumes/`.

Now, we can set our passwords for the MySQL instance (replace "password" with something more appropriate):

```
fly secrets set MYSQL_PASSWORD=password MYSQL_ROOT_
PASSWORD=root_password
```

Throughout this process, Fly.io has created a `fly.toml` file for its applications (one for our web application in the project's root directory and another for MySQL in the `fly-mysql` directory). This is similar to Heroku's `Procfile` or CloudFlare's `wrangler.toml` file. Within the fly.toml file we will want to replace its contents, after the first line (the application's name) or starting from the `kill_signal` line, with the following:

```
kill_signal = "SIGINT"
kill_timeout = 5

[mounts]
  source="mysqldata"
  destination="/data"

[env]
  MYSQL_DATABASE = "avalon_airlines"
  MYSQL_USER = "avalon_airlines"

[build]
  image = "mysql:5.7"

[experimental]
  cmd = [
    "--default-authentication-plugin",
    "mysql_native_password",
    "--datadir",
    "/data/mysql"
  ]
```

After modifying the file's contents, we can scale our MySQL application to have 256 MB of RAM and deploy the MySQL instance:

```
fly scale memory 256
fly deploy
```

Now, going back to the project's root directory, we can add a DATABSE_URL environment secret to our web application's Fly.io configuration by running the following command:

```
flyctl secrets set DATABASE_URL=mysql://avalon_airlines:<YOUR
PASSWORD>@<YOUR MYSQL'S APPLICATION NAME>.internal/avalon_
airlines
```

Replace YOUR_PASSWORD with the password that was previously set for the MySQL's application's MYSQL_PASSWORD secret. Your MySQL's application name should be available in the fly-mysql/fly.toml file marked with the app key.

> **Note**
>
> If you lose track of your application's names, the Fly.io CLI provides a way to list all of your account's application using the flyctl apps list command.

We will need to make some modifications to the package.json file. Since the application's builder is using Heroku's buildpacks, the application will be built with whatever the latest **Long-Term Supported** (**LTS**) Node.js version exist. The builder will also run the start script by default which currently uses nodemon. We can ensure the application is built with the proper Node.js version, and removing the nodemon dependency by replacing the start script within package.json to look like the following:

```
"scripts": {
  "start": "node index.js",
  "dev": "nodemon index.js"
},
"engines": {
  "node": "16.x"
},
```

Now, for when we are developing the application locally, we will want to execute npm run dev instead of npm run start.

> **Note**
>
> More information, and caveats, for Heroku's Node.js buildpack can be found at https://devcenter.heroku.com/articles/nodejs-support.

From the Avalon Airlines project, we would need to open and modify the `config/index.js` file and replace the production object with the appropriate database connection values:

```
"production": {
    "use_env_variable": "DATABASE_URL",
    "dialect": "mysql"
}
```

Fly.io will deploy within a container cluster that exposes ports from a dynamic range. Due to this stipulation, we are required to modify the `app.listen(3000, …)` at the bottom of `index.js`:

```
app.listen(process.env.PORT || 3000, function () {
    console.log("> express server has started");
});
```

This will use the PORT environment variable, and default to a value of 3000 if the environment variable is not found, exposing our Express application properly on Fly.io's ecosystem. There is one more change on the project root directory within the `fly.toml` file we will need to replace the `[env]` block with the following:

```
[env]
  PORT = "8080"
  NODE_ENV = "production"
```

Everything else should remain the same, and now, we can deploy and open our application:

```
flyctl deploy
flyctl open
```

> **Note**
>
> You may receive a similar error as, "Cannot find module 'sequelize'," this can be from a third-party application dependency such as Admin.js. As a temporarily solution we can manually install, and save, the original Sequelize library by entering `npm i sequelize` into your terminal within the projects directory and re-deploy your application.

You may notice that the website looks a little bare, we can head over to the /admin dashboard route and start populating our airplane inventory and flight schedules. Once that is done, we can start processing and booking tickets for Avalon Airlines!

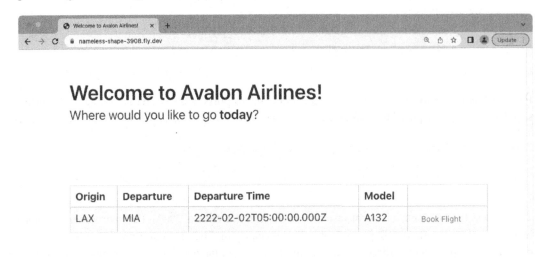

Figure 10.7 – The Avalon Airlines homepage with a flight scheduled!

Summary

In this chapter, we went through the process of adding a frontend page with the ability to generate a list of flight schedules and create boarding tickets. We also learned how to deploy our application to a cloud application environment.

Congratulations! We have completed the process of becoming familiar with Sequelize to deploying a Sequelize-based web application. In a real-world scenario, we would want to make a few more adjustments, such as securely storing database credentials, setting up transactional emails, adding more pages, processing credit cards, and having an actual seating inventory management system. At this point, the rest is up to you and only the sky is the limit! Hopefully, this will be a satisfying start for you! It certainly should be, because the Avalon Airlines board members are pleased so far, and they've decided to fund our next round.

Index

Packt.com

Subscribe to our online digital library for full access to over 7,000 books and videos, as well as industry leading tools to help you plan your personal development and advance your career. For more information, please visit our website.

Why subscribe?

- Spend less time learning and more time coding with practical eBooks and Videos from over 4,000 industry professionals

- Improve your learning with Skill Plans built especially for you

- Get a free eBook or video every month

- Fully searchable for easy access to vital information

- Copy and paste, print, and bookmark content

Did you know that Packt offers eBook versions of every book published, with PDF and ePub files available? You can upgrade to the eBook version at packt.com and as a print book customer, you are entitled to a discount on the eBook copy. Get in touch with us at customercare@packtpub. com for more details.

At www.packt.com, you can also read a collection of free technical articles, sign up for a range of free newsletters, and receive exclusive discounts and offers on Packt books and eBooks.

Other Books You May Enjoy

If you enjoyed this book, you may be interested in these other books by Packt:

Node.js Web Development - Fifth Edition

David Herron

ISBN: 978-1-83898-757-2

- Install and use Node.js 14 and Express 4.17 for both web development and deployment
- Implement RESTful web services using the Restify framework
- Develop, test, and deploy microservices using Docker, Docker Swarm, and Node.js, on AWS EC2 using Terraform
- Get up to speed with using data storage engines such as MySQL, SQLite3, and MongoDB
- Test your web applications using unit testing with Mocha, and headless browser testing with Puppeteer
- Implement HTTPS using Let's Encrypt and enhance application security with Helmet

Full-Stack React Projects - Second Edition

Shama Hoque

ISBN: 978-1-83921-541-4

- Extend a basic MERN-based application to build a variety of applications
- Add real-time communication capabilities with Socket.IO
- Implement data visualization features for React applications using Victory
- Develop media streaming applications using MongoDB GridFS
- Improve SEO for your MERN apps by implementing server-side rendering with data
- Implement user authentication and authorization using JSON web tokens
- Set up and use React 360 to develop user interfaces with VR capabilities
- Make your MERN stack applications reliable and scalable with industry best practices

Packt is searching for authors like you

If you're interested in becoming an author for Packt, please visit `authors.packtpub.com` and apply today. We have worked with thousands of developers and tech professionals, just like you, to help them share their insight with the global tech community. You can make a general application, apply for a specific hot topic that we are recruiting an author for, or submit your own idea.

Share Your Thoughts

Now you've finished *Supercharging Node.js Applications with Sequelize*, we'd love to hear your thoughts! Scan the QR code below to go straight to the Amazon review page for this book and share your feedback or leave a review on the site that you purchased it from.

`https://packt.link/r/1801811555`

Your review is important to us and the tech community and will help us make sure we're delivering excellent quality content.

Download a free PDF copy of this book

Thanks for purchasing this book!

Do you like to read on the go but are unable to carry your print books everywhere?

Is your eBook purchase not compatible with the device of your choice?

Don't worry, now with every Packt book you get a DRM-free PDF version of that book at no cost.

Read anywhere, any place, on any device. Search, copy, and paste code from your favorite technical books directly into your application.

The perks don't stop there, you can get exclusive access to discounts, newsletters, and great free content in your inbox daily

Follow these simple steps to get the benefits:

1. Scan the QR code or visit the link below

https://packt.link/free-ebook/9781801811552

2. Submit your proof of purchase

3. That's it! We'll send your free PDF and other benefits to your email directly

Made in the USA
Monee, IL
25 January 2024

52332360R00149